T0265780

TAMING THE RISK
HURRICANE

PREPARING FOR MAJOR
BUSINESS DISRUPTION

David Hillson

BK
Berrett–Koehler Publishers, Inc.

Berrett-Koehler Publishers, Inc.
1333 Broadway, Suite 1000
Oakland, CA 94612-1921
Tel: (510) 817-2277   Fax: (510) 817-2278   www.bkconnection.com

Ordering Information

Quantity sales. Special discounts are available on quantity purchases by corporations, associations, and others. For details, contact the "Special Sales Department" at the Berrett-Koehler address above.

Individual sales. Berrett-Koehler publications are available through most bookstores. They can also be ordered directly from Berrett-Koehler: Tel: (800) 929-2929; Fax: (802) 864-7626; www.bkconnection.com.

Orders for college textbook / course adoption use. Please contact Berrett-Koehler: Tel: (800) 929-2929; Fax: (802) 864-7626.

Distributed to the U.S. trade and internationally by Penguin Random House Publisher Services.

Berrett-Koehler and the BK logo are registered trademarks of Berrett-Koehler Publishers, Inc.

Printed in the United States of America

Berrett-Koehler books are printed on long-lasting acid-free paper. When it is available, we choose paper that has been manufactured by environmentally responsible processes. These may include using trees grown in sustainable forests, incorporating recycled paper, minimizing chlorine in bleaching, or recycling the energy produced at the paper mill.

Library of Congress Cataloging-in-Publication Data
Names: Hillson, David, 1955– author.
Title: Taming the risk hurricane : preparing for major business disruption / David Hillson.
Description: First edition. | Oakland, CA : Berrett-Koehler Publishers, [2022] | Includes
    bibliographical references and index.
Identifiers: LCCN 2022004807 (print) | LCCN 2022004808 (ebook) | ISBN 9781523000494
    (paperback) | ISBN 9781523000500 (pdf) | ISBN 9781523000517 (epub) |
    ISBN 9781523000524
Subjects: LCSH: Risk management.
Classification: LCC HD61 .H4776 2022 (print) | LCC HD61 (ebook) | DDC 658.15/5—
    dc23/eng/20220318
LC record available at https://lccn.loc.gov/2022004807
LC ebook record available at https://lccn.loc.gov/2022004808

First Edition

30 29 28 27 26 25 24 23 22   10 9 8 7 6 5 4 3 2 1

Book production: Westchester Publishing Services
Cover design: Peggy Archambault

Contents

Figures and Tables

FIGURES

TABLES

Foreword

Frank P. Saladis, PMP,
PMI Fellow

For many people, the mere mention of the word "hurricane" conjures up thoughts of devastation, destruction, and loss. The English word comes from the mid-sixteenth century Spanish huracán, which was most likely taken from the indigenous Taino people of the Caribbean, for whom Hurikán was "god of evil," who in turn derived it from the Mayan Hurakán "god of wind and storm."

I've personally witnessed the destructive force of two hurricanes: Katrina in New Orleans and Sandy in New York City. I was in New Orleans in 2005 as Katrina approached. As I toured the city the night before the hurricane made landfall, I saw how unprepared the city was. My plane was the last to leave on the morning that the hurricane hit, but I returned to help build a house after the storm. I was also in New York City during Hurricane Sandy in 2012, and I saw the devastation for myself. After the storm, I volunteered to help people who had been displaced and spoke at a fundraiser for hurricane victims. Those experiences convinced me that plans, preparation, and readiness to address the inevitable disruption are essential.

It is safe to assume that most people have seen the effects of a hurricane through the media, even if they have not experienced one in person. I'm sure that those scenes of disruption and destruction will have raised this question in the minds of many: "What if it happens here?" The formation of a hurricane and its projected path immediately initiates thoughts of risk, with the need for preparation and making plans for protection and mitigation.

The hurricane is also a great analogy for describing the impact of risk in the business environment, as well as in personal daily life. That "god of wind and storm" seems to be lurking around today's business environment, preparing ever-present risk events and just waiting to unleash them and wreak havoc on large and small businesses alike.

In this book, David Hillson uses the term "Risk Hurricane" to describe circumstances of extreme risk exposure in business that lead to major disruption. Today's businesses exist in a world of VUCA (volatility, uncertainty, complexity, and ambiguity), which is getting a lot of attention. Here too in this environment of rapid and intense change, the question "What if it happens here?" is being asked, highlighted by the disruptive tendencies of new players and business models. Today's business leaders are compelled to focus much more on the potential impact of risk and create a culture of "extreme risk awareness" to ensure their organizations will be able to withstand the force of a Risk Hurricane.

Taming the Risk Hurricane explores the nature of the Risk Hurricane through an extended analogy woven into each chapter from preconditions to post-event recovery. Along the way, the book develops a well-defined risk management approach and drives the need for total organizational risk awareness. It acts as a stimulant for business leaders to remain conscious of risk, encouraging them to ensure that everyone becomes an advocate for risk management.

From my firsthand experience with a deadly hurricane, I recognize that *Taming the Risk Hurricane* is a call to action for all business leaders and public servants. We all know there is uncertainty in life and in business, but not all those uncertainties are equally significant. This book provides a structured thought process to help us determine when we need to take action and how we can condition our organizations to become highly risk aware. Risk awareness should be considered a very positive aspect of an organization's culture that will lead to better and more business-focused decisions. Equally important, it helps the organization to prepare for and withstand the potentially dangerous and disruptive side of risk that a Risk Hurricane represents.

As a business leader, your goal is to enable your business to weather the storm and maintain business continuity through demonstrated leadership. Consider this book to be your guide to establishing a highly practical and effective risk management approach. In this world of emphasis on outcomes, the lessons learned from this book not only will provide the foundation for protection from an oncoming Risk Hurricane but also will help you to minimize the impact and recovery period of a major risk event. *Taming the Risk Hurricane* is an essential resource for business leaders and their risk management colleagues, emphasizing the need for continuous vigilance in an often-overlooked area of responsibility.

Prologue

Hurricanes always attract attention. As the most extreme of weather events, they are beloved by the media and feared by those in their path, while onlookers from further afield watch with fascination. The names of the most destructive hurricanes pass into legend: Andrew (1992), Mitch (1998), Katrina (2005), Sandy (2012), Maria and Irma (2017), Dorian (2019), and more. Their immediate impacts are felt in terms of lives lost, homes destroyed, and businesses wiped out, with longer-term damage to infrastructure, local communities, and mental well-being.

Corporate crises also hit the headlines and have their own morbid appeal. When a prominent organization is overtaken by extreme events and subsequently crashes spectacularly, the media splash the story, investors panic, stock markets react, suppliers go out of business, competitors gloat, and customers worry. The fascination is only heightened if the crisis was caused by foreseeable-but-unforeseen risk: accounting fraud at Enron (2001), Lehman Brothers' investment in mortgage debt (2008), VW cheating on emissions testing (2015), the miniaturized blood tests of Theranos (2018).

What's the connection between hurricanes and corporate crisis? This book provides the answer.

Taming the Risk Hurricane: Preparing for Major Business Disruption is an extended metaphor, comparing two unrelated things and using characteristics of one to unlock useful insights about the other.

We use the meteorological phenomenon of the hurricane to draw out important points about the effects of extreme uncertainty on organizations, and in the process of comparison, we develop the concept of the Risk Hurricane.

Joseph W. Mayo first used the term "Risk Hurricane" in his book *Cultural Calamity*: *Culture-Driven Risk Management Disasters and How to Avoid Them* (Mayo, 2017). Although Joe coined the Risk Hurricane phrase, his book was specifically about how organizations are exposed to culturally induced risk. He explains four cultural warning signs of a developing Risk Hurricane (Mayo, n.d.):

- Normalized deviance—viewing problems as unavoidable
- Rejection—refusing to take note of vulnerabilities or noncompliances
- Deception—intentionally diverting attention away from growing risk exposure
- Risk normalization—simplified risk analysis and reporting, resulting in loss of information

But when I saw the term "Risk Hurricane," my curiosity was piqued. In what other ways is a critical corporate crisis like a hurricane? What does risk have to do with it? Why is this an appropriate comparison? In addition to the cultural aspects highlighted by Joe, what else can we learn from the idea? Joe has kindly allowed me to take his original idea and run with it, and this book is the result. Building on Joe's work, here we use the power of analogy to develop a generic model of corporate crisis, not limited to those that are induced by culture.

The problem with extended comparisons is that they often stretch beyond the realms of credulity. This book takes as its starting point a simple idea: ***The Risk Hurricane describes circumstances of extreme risk exposure in business that lead to major disruption***. The causes and consequences of meteorological hurricanes have parallels to the way uncontrolled risk exposure can develop in organizations. Many different people are involved in some way when a natural hurricane occurs, just as there are a range of stakeholders involved when an organization experiences extreme risk-based disruption. Hurricanes can be predicted, prepared for, and recovered from, and the same is true of the Risk Hurricane. We don't stray too far beyond these comparisons, and hopefully the analogy bears up under examination.

Another problem with use of analogy is that there's a temptation to focus on the wrong part of the comparison. If "A is like B," it's too easy to become fascinated by the details of A when the purpose of the comparison is to expose new insights about B. A natural hurricane is a serious matter and it deserves serious attention. Professional meteorologists understand the complexities of weather systems in a way that the rest of us can't, and we depend on their expertise. Each chapter of this book starts by outlining an aspect of natural hurricanes, and much more could be said. But the book is not about hurricanes ("A"); it is about extreme risk exposure in businesses ("B"). Using natural hurricanes in this way is not to trivialize them or to minimize the severe impact they have on people's lives and livelihoods. But here, we need to maintain focus on our purpose: to use the comparison to develop helpful insights about risk and its management.

Parts of this book were written on the beautiful Caribbean island of Antigua, in a part of the world that regularly experiences hurricanes. When I started work on the book, the Bahamas were recovering from the recent devastating passage of Hurricane Dorian, one of the worst Category 5 Atlantic hurricanes on record. Fortunately, my visit was uneventful, but the location helped me to focus on the reality behind the natural side of the analogy. I hope the book will also concentrate minds on the existence and importance of extreme risk exposure, helping many organizations to foresee potentially disruptive corporate crises and giving them the tools to face the Risk Hurricane with maximum preparedness and resilience.

ONE

Introducing the Risk Hurricane

This book presents an extended analogy, holding two dissimilar things in parallel so that similarities and differences can provide new insights. Starting from the meteorological phenomenon of the hurricane, we'll explore key characteristics of extreme risk exposure in business, explaining how it arises, how it can be predicted, how its effects can be mitigated or managed, and how an organization can recover after an extreme risk event.

This chapter sets the scene with some definitions and context for what follows.

THE HURRICANE AS ANALOGY

In 1805 Commander Francis Beaufort of the British Royal Navy developed a scale to describe the range of wind conditions that might be encountered by shipping. The *Beaufort Wind Force Scale* has since been adapted and extended, and it has become a de facto standard, with its terms and definitions universally accepted and used. The key elements of the Beaufort Wind Force Scale are summarized in Table 1.1, defining each level in terms of wind speed and wave height. The full scale also includes descriptions of conditions on land and at sea for each level.

Within the structure of the Beaufort scale, the hurricane represents the most severe level of storm that might be encountered. Even then, meteorologists felt the need for more granularity at the top end, and the Beaufort scale has been extended to describe different categories of hurricane. This is discussed in more detail in Chapter 3.

Table 1.1: The Beaufort Wind Force Scale (extract)

Beaufort number	Description	Wind speed		Wave height	
		km/h	mph	m	ft
0	Calm	< 1	< 1	0	0
1	Light air	1–5	1–3	0.1	0.33
2	Light breeze	6–11	3–7	0.2	0.66
3	Gentle breeze	12–19	8–12	0.6	2
4	Moderate breeze	20–28	13–17	1	3.3
5	Fresh breeze	29–38	18–24	2	6.6
6	Strong breeze	39–49	25–30	3	9.9
7	Moderate gale	50–61	31–38	4	13.1
8	Gale	62–74	39–46	5.5	18
9	Strong gale	75–88	47–54	7	23
10	Storm	89–102	55–63	9	29.5
11	Violent storm	103–117	64–72	11.5	37.7
12	Hurricane	≥ 118	≥ 73	≥ 14	≥ 46

Given their unique position as the top-ranking type of storm system and their potential to wreak havoc on those communities unfortunate enough to experience one, it's not surprising that hurricanes receive a lot of attention from professional meteorologists, academics, the media, and the public. This has led to increased appreciation of how they form, what drives their intensity, how they might be predicted, how to respond when one is heading your way, and how to recover afterward. This level of detailed understanding makes the natural hurricane eminently suitable as the starting point for an analogy.

DEFINING THE RISK HURRICANE

With the natural hurricane as the illustrative half of our analogy, what is the matching half for which we hope to gain a new perspective and new insights?

Today's business world is characterized by volatility, uncertainty, complexity, and ambiguity (embodied in the VUCA acronym), with high rates of change and the emergence of disruptive new players and business models:

- **V.** Markets vary widely in times of stress and uncertainty, as measured by the VIX (Volatility Index), but volatility is also found widely elsewhere in the business environment, including raw material prices, labor market availability, and customer demand.
- **U.** Uncertainty is essentially driven by lack of predictability, where causal factors are unclear.
- **C.** Increased interdependence, interconnectedness, and hidden linkages characterize situations of rising complexity, where future behavior of systems is difficult or impossible to analyze from past performance.
- **A.** The explosion in data and information results in high levels of ambiguity, making it increasingly challenging to know what's going on with any degree of accuracy.

Each VUCA element alone can create problems for businesses, but for many organizations, the combination of VUCA factors working together generates an unprecedented level of strategic risk exposure that presents an existential challenge. Businesses that are unable to handle such extreme risk exposure will go under, while those that survive will necessarily demonstrate a high degree of flexibility and resilience, giving them competitive advantage and the ability to thrive where others fail.

Many organizations rely on standard risk management processes to protect them from extreme existential risk exposure. But perhaps this confidence is misplaced?

Risk management has become a standard part of the strategic toolkit in recent years, providing senior leaders with a forward-looking radar to scan the future and give early warning of approaching threats and opportunities. Risk has entered the language of the boardroom and is no longer limited to subsidiary levels such as technical, safety, reputation, insurance, business continuity, projects, or operations. Leading organizations have become adept at risk-based decision-making, understanding and expressing their strategic risk appetite through measurable risk thresholds that drive the risk-taking activities of the whole enterprise (Hillson & Murray-Webster, 2012; Murray-Webster & Hillson, 2021).

However, even these best-in-class organizations can falter in the face of extreme risk exposure that is beyond anything they've previously experienced. This intense degree of uncertainty doesn't happen every day, and routine risk management approaches aren't designed to deal with it. Special circumstances demand special responses, and extreme risk exposure requires very careful handling.

This is where the concept of the Risk Hurricane comes in. *The Risk Hurricane describes circumstances of extreme risk exposure in business that lead to major disruption*. It is caused largely by predictable factors but characterized by sustained unpredictability and severe impact once it develops. If we can learn to predict a Risk Hurricane, to prepare for it effectively, and to survive its effects, then our organizations will be well placed to address the challenge of extreme risk exposure, if/when we are unfortunate enough to face it. While traditional risk management processes can form part of the response to a Risk Hurricane, they are insufficient on their own. The chapters that follow provide additional techniques and approaches that are better suited to addressing extreme risk exposure, complementing more routine risk management techniques, and providing the required level of robust protection.

RISK BASICS

The "hurricane" part of the Risk Hurricane is the basis for the analogy used throughout this book. But what about the "risk" part? In many ways, this element is more important, as it defines the area of interest about which we want to draw inferences and insights. There are many *circumstances that can cause major disruption to businesses*, but the Risk Hurricane is distinguished by its focus on circumstances of *extreme risk exposure*.

To understand the nature of the Risk Hurricane, we first have to understand the nature of risk. *Risk is not the same as uncertainty.* There are innumerable uncertainties in the world, but we do not count them all as risks. All risks are uncertain, but not all uncertainties are risks. Risk is therefore a subset of uncertainty. We need a filter to determine which uncertainties must be understood and managed as risks. This filter is embodied in a simple proto-definition: "Risk is uncertainty that matters." The vast majority of uncertainties do not matter, and we can safely ignore them.

What matters is defined by our *objectives*; these describe what is "at risk." We can therefore expand our proto-definition of risk to be a little more specific: "Risk is uncertainty that, if it occurs, would affect objectives." This most basic definition of risk is reflected in all current risk management standards and guidelines, from the international ISO 31000:2018 *Risk management—Guidelines* (International Organization for Standardization, 2018) to national and sector-specific examples. The level of objective determines the type of risk: strategic risk would affect strategic objectives; operational risk would affect operational objectives; personal risk would affect personal objectives; and so on.

One more basic principle of risk must be stated here, as it is directly relevant to the Risk Hurricane. "Risk is uncertainty that, if it occurs, would affect objectives," but that effect could be either negative, or positive, or both. The concept of risk incudes *threat* (uncertainty with negative impact), *opportunity* (uncertainty with positive impact), *variability* (uncertainty with uncertain impact), and *ambiguity* (uncertainty with unknown impact).

This means that risk includes uncertain future events that can be foreseen with some degree of accuracy, allowing you to predict them and prepare for them. But risk also covers uncertainties that are harder to anticipate, whose impact is often unclear, which makes them much more difficult to address proactively in advance (though not impossible). Risk management must cover predictable risks (known-unknowns and knowable-unknowns) as well as emergent risks (unknown-unknowns and unknowable-unknowns), dealing with uncertainty wherever and however it arises.

As a consequence, *risk exposure* describes the totality of the effects that uncertainty might have on our ability to achieve our objectives. The *"extreme risk exposure"* associated with the Risk Hurricane reflects a degree of uncertainty that could have an existential impact on the business. Of course, the definition of "extreme" will differ from one organization to another, and it is vital for the leaders of each business to have a clear view of "how much risk is too much risk," embodied in their strategic *risk capacity*.

Once we know what we mean by risk and what level of risk exposure counts as "extreme" to our business, we can proceed to find and manage those uncertainties that matter to us. Simple principles underpin the *risk management process*, which in essence requires us to ask and answer eight basic questions:

1. What are we trying to achieve? (strategic objective-setting)
2. What might affect our ability to achieve these objectives? (risk identification)
3. Which of those are most important? (risk assessment and prioritization)
4. What can we do about them? (risk response planning)
5. Having done what we planned, did it work? (risk response implementation, risk review)
6. Whom should we tell? (risk communication and reporting)
7. What's changed? (risk updates)
8. What should we do differently next time? (learning risk-related lessons)

Most organizations will be familiar with this process, and you're probably already implementing some form of it within your business. The level of implementation will vary widely from one company to another, depending on the size and nature of the business. Some may have a full enterprise-wide risk management (ERM) approach, perhaps following an established framework such as COSO (Committee of Sponsoring Organizations of the Treadway Commission, 2017), where others may have a more informal approach (for example Chapman, 2011; Taylor, 2014). The form of your process matters less than the fact that you've adopted a structured approach to managing the risks faced by your business and that you're implementing that consistently across all levels of the organization.

Armed with a firm understanding of the importance of risk to your business, as well as a sense of where the limits of acceptable risk exposure lie, you'll be better equipped to spot an approaching Risk Hurricane and deal with it effectively.

BOOK OUTLINE

Throughout the following chapters, we use known facts about natural hurricanes to generate new insights about the Risk Hurricane, as outlined in Table 1.2. Each of Chapters 2 through 7 unpacks one aspect of the hurricane analogy, starting with a brief description of the characteristics of a natural hurricane, leading into an exploration of comparable factors relevant to the effects of extreme risk exposure on business. These chapters also each include a short case study to illustrate one aspect of the Risk Hurricane, drawing on well-known examples of extreme risk exposure from the public domain.

The book closes with a final chapter summarizing lessons to be learned by any business that wants or needs to prepare to face extreme risk exposure, with a call to action outlining the practical and strategic steps that must be taken to tame the Risk Hurricane.

Table 1.2: The Risk Hurricane analogy

Opening analogy	The Risk Hurricane (extreme risk exposure that leads to major business disruption)	is like	A natural hurricane (the most severe and devastating level of storm)
Analogous areas Aspects of the natural hurricane offering useful insights into the Risk Hurricane	PRECONDITIONS [Chapter 2]: How and why a hurricane forms		
	POTENCY [Chapter 3]: Drivers and measures of hurricane force		
	PEOPLE [Chapter 4]: Interested parties involved in a hurricane		
	PREDICTION [Chapter 5]: Forecasting and communication		
	PREPAREDNESS [Chapter 6]: How to get ready before the hurricane arrives		
	POST-EVENT RECOVERY [Chapter 7]: How to recover after the hurricane has passed		

TERMINOLOGY FOOTNOTE

The term "hurricane" is only used for storms that occur in the North Atlantic and Northeast Pacific Oceans. The same type of storm in the Northwest Pacific Ocean is known as a "typhoon," and in the South Pacific and Indian Oceans it's a "cyclone." For simplicity, in this book we only talk about hurricanes, but the same principles apply to typhoons and cyclones. We hope readers from these other regions of the world will understand and accept this simplification. The Risk Typhoon and Risk Cyclone are equally relevant analogies, and what we say about the Risk Hurricane is just as relevant wherever you are in the world.

TWO

Preconditions

Watching the formation of a natural hurricane is a truly awesome experience. Meteorologists can put together animations of photos from space to show how these monster storms arise apparently from nowhere, and the sight inevitably inspires strong emotions. The most powerful weather system our planet can produce seems to come literally out of thin air.

Of course, the reality of how hurricanes form is quite different. They don't come from nowhere; instead, there are clear preconditions that must be present in order to set in motion the sequence of events that eventually produces a full-strength hurricane. By understanding and monitoring these preconditions, people who might be affected by a hurricane can maximize the time available for preparation and protection.

In the same way, as we look for insights to help us understand extreme risk exposure in business, it would be helpful to identify the necessary preconditions for a Risk Hurricane. This chapter offers three influences that work together to allow a Risk Hurricane to form. We characterize 21 factors in the *external environment* that create uncertainty for businesses, describe the elements of *risk culture* and *risk mindset* that make an organization vulnerable to risk, and highlight the important role of *change* as a trigger of extreme risk exposure.

NATURAL HURRICANE PRECONDITIONS

All hurricanes follow the same life cycle, described below and illustrated in Figure 2.1:

- Hurricanes form in the tropics (between latitudes 8° and 20°), over a warm ocean where the water temperature is above 26.5°C. The heat and moisture from this warm water provide the energy source for what follows. The initial stage is known as a *tropical wave*, which is a westward-moving area of low air pressure.
- The warm ocean water evaporates and rises in the low air pressure area, and it is replaced by colder air, which in turn is heated and rises, generating strong gusty winds. Moist air condenses to form thunderclouds with heavy rain, releasing latent heat energy. This combination of conditions is called a *tropical disturbance*.
- If ocean temperatures remain high enough, the cycle will continue, leading to faster flows of rising and falling air, with sustained wind speeds of up to 38 mph (Beaufort force 7), known as a *tropical depression*.
- The ongoing cycle of air flows produces large storm clouds, which begin to spin due to the Earth's rotation and the Coriolis effect, causing the storm to become organized. The spiraling wind increases in speed as it moves inward toward the center of the vortex, moving up through the Beaufort scale from force 8 to 11, with sustained wind speeds of 39 to 72 mph. During this stage it becomes a *tropical storm* and is eligible to be named.
- Sustained wind speeds rising above 72 mph indicate that a full *hurricane* has developed. The hurricane can continue to grow in size and strength while it remains over warm water, but it will begin to dissipate when it moves over land or colder ocean waters. When sustained wind speeds fall below 73 mph, the hurricane is downgraded to a tropical storm, and its life is effectively over.

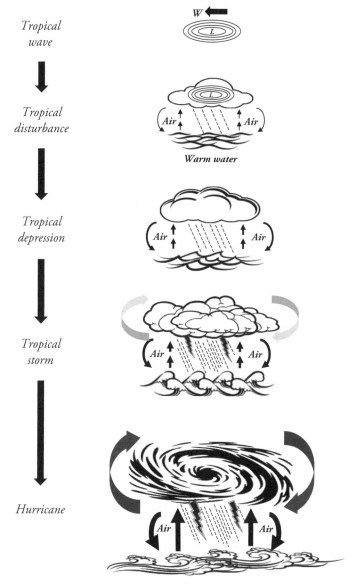

Figure 2.1: *Stages in hurricane development*

As we follow these stages in the development of a hurricane, we can identify three necessary preconditions:

1. Warm ocean water
2. Low air pressure
3. Circulating wind vortices

Each of these three factors alone is insufficient to produce a hurricane, but in combination the outcome is guaranteed. Turning to our analogy, let's consider whether there are similar necessary preconditions that must be in place for a Risk Hurricane to develop.

RISK HURRICANE PRECONDITIONS

Where does extreme risk exposure come from? Does it arise out of the blue, without warning, appearing fully formed in a business or organization? Although it might feel that way to people affected by a Risk Hurricane, in fact extreme risk exposure is the result of the conjunction of several factors in a synergistic manner, each strengthening the other and resulting in ever-increasing self-sustaining uncertainty and severely disruptive impact.

We've described three preconditions that are required in order for a natural hurricane to form. In the same way, it's possible to identify three preconditions for the Risk Hurricane that cause extreme risk exposure in business:

1. External environment
2. Internal environment
3. Rate of change

EXTERNAL ENVIRONMENT

There are many sources of uncertainty in today's business environment that can contribute to the risk exposure encountered by an organization. A range of mnemonics have been developed to help business leaders remember these factors, many of which are confusingly similar, including:

- PESTLE—Political, Economic, Social, Technological, Legal, Environmental
- STEEPLE—as PESTLE, with the addition of Ethics
- PESTLIED—as PESTLE, with the addition of International (or Informational) and Demographic
- InSPECT—Innovation, Social, Political, Economic, Communications, Technology

- SPECTRUM—Socio-cultural, Political, Economic, Competitive, Technology, Regulatory/Legal, Uncertainty/Risk, Market
- TECOP—Technical, Environmental, Commercial, Operational, Political
- VUCA—Volatility, Uncertainty, Complexity, Ambiguity

These factors are consolidated in Figure 2.2. Most of them are external to the organization, but some relate to the type of business being undertaken (Operational, for example).

We've seen that warm ocean water provides the environment within which the early stages of a hurricane can develop. In a similar way, sources of uncertainty in the external business environment promote the formation of a Risk Hurricane. Warm water acts as the energy source for a tropical storm, which is driven by heat and moisture. The warmer the water, the more energy is available to fuel the storm. Similarly, when external sources of uncertainty in the business environment are strong, conditions favor the development of extreme risk exposure. This is explored briefly for

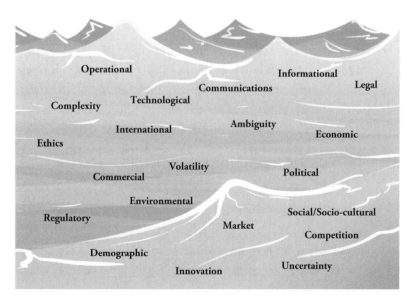

Figure 2.2: *Sources of uncertainty in external business environment*

each of the factors in Figure 2.2 (presented in alphabetical order for ease of reference):

- *Ambiguity.* Ambiguity arises from incomplete understanding of crucial aspects of a situation. High levels of ambiguity mean that business leaders are unable to plan with confidence. As a result, increased risk is built into strategic and tactical plans, which will have to be modified as ambiguity reduces and things become clearer.
- *Commercial.* Increasingly complex forms of contract result in the possibility of an organization taking on commitments and obligations that are onerous or difficult/impossible to deliver. This is exacerbated by extended supply chains with multiple contractual boundaries and interfaces, which are becoming more common in a globalized business environment. When contractual commitments involve multiple regulatory regimes, the situation becomes even more risky.
- *Communications.* The importance of clear communication is well understood, but it is not always well practiced. If communication is compromised, incomplete, or misleading, then subsequent decisions and actions will be built on insecure foundations, and risk exposure will be higher.
- *Competition.* The actions of competitors in shared market space can never be fully known or predicted in advance, which represents a significant source of uncertainty for most businesses. Existing competitors may launch new or improved products or services, change their pricing strategy, undergo mergers or acquisitions or demergers, launch an aggressive recruitment campaign targeting our workforce demographic, or even exit our market altogether. In addition, new players may enter our market space, perhaps with disruptive customer offerings or business models or technological solutions.
- *Complexity.* At first sight, this factor relates more to the nature of the business of the organization rather than to the external environment. However, in addition, there are often external complexities that can give rise to significant uncertainty for a business,

including market structures, technological or scientific theories and discoveries, supply chain interconnectivity, and so on. One key characteristic of complexity is unpredictability: simple cause-and-effect relationships rarely exist in complex settings.

- *Demographic.* Populations are becoming increasingly volatile, including at national and ethnic levels, with large-scale migrations, alterations in age profiles, and changes in social mobility and related expectations. The demographic factor also includes generational issues, as the people who make up our workforce, management, client base, and competitors transition from Baby Boomers, through Gen X and Millennials, to Gen Z and the Alpha Generation. The impact of these generational changes is hard to predict and may invalidate some aspects of existing business models.

- *Economic.* The economic environment is clearly a significant factor in the health of any business, including availability of loans, interest rates, exchange rates, insurance, market performance, share values, tariffs, and so on. Both the macro- and microeconomic circumstances can change with little or no warning and can generate substantial risk exposure for a business.

- *Environmental.* The natural environment can influence businesses both directly and indirectly, especially following the rise of populist activism. Environmental factors have a direct effect on businesses that depend on natural resources, or where operations interact with the natural environment. This is often thought to be limited to the extractive and energy industries, but other sectors can also be indirectly affected by environmental issues, especially if activists perceive a link between the environment and the products or conduct of a business. Organizations that directly impact the environment are generally aware of potentially disruptive issues and build mitigating responses into their actions. But indirect impacts arising from environmental issues can strike other businesses without warning, leading to significant reputational and operational impacts.

- *Ethics.* Business ethics has received increased attention in recent years, in response to a number of scandals in various industries.

While ethics forms part of the internal culture of an organization, external ethical issues can be raised unexpectedly, increasing risk exposure for the business.

- *Informational.* Information is an important direct resource for many organizations, but enhanced attention to data privacy and cybersecurity has led to increased risk exposure in this area for a wide range of businesses and industry sectors. Wherever customer data are collected for valid business reasons, the organization has a duty to keep them secure and use them only for specified purposes.

- *Innovation.* All innovation involves uncertainty, as the organization seeks to do existing things better or to do new things that are useful and profitable. There is no guarantee that innovation will produce results, even when it is undertaken incrementally or in an agile manner. Any business that relies significantly on innovation for growth or success is naturally exposed to risk in this area. In addition to internal innovation as a source of risk, aspects of innovation in the external environment can increase our risk exposure. For example, competitors may innovate in our area of business, and technological developments might affect our operations, processes, or products.

- *International.* The business environment is increasingly global in the structure of transnational corporations, the reach of supply chains, and the client base. This naturally introduces multiple sources of uncertainty, including language, culture, business practices, regulations, forms of contract, and so on. The international dimension can change rapidly, leading to high levels of risk exposure for businesses operating in this context.

- *Legal.* In most countries, the laws governing businesses are fairly complex, and they often require interpretation by legal advisers. This source of uncertainty can be significant if key strategic decisions depend on legal opinion that might be challenged.

- *Market.* Market forces are often hard to understand and predict, with unknown factors driving demand, market share, or growth potential. Even the best analysts are often behind the curve, reacting to the latest market shift instead of anticipating it. For many businesses, the state of the market presents a major source of uncertainty that can contribute significantly to high levels of risk exposure.

- [*Operational.* This heading is included in just one of the risk source mnemonics (TECOP) and properly belongs to the internal workings of the organization, rather than being an element of its external environment.]
- *Political.* In many countries, the political landscape plays an important part in setting the context for business. Changes in government following elections might result in wholesale transitions in the political arena, but a simple change of minister can produce policy moves that affect our business significantly. This is likely to have a particularly strong impact on those organizations working in the public sector or engaged in public-private partnership (PPP) contracts.
- *Regulatory.* Some industries are highly regulated, and any change in the regulatory regime can have a major effect on business performance for these organizations. Such changes may arise in response to high-profile incidents or new international agreements and are often hard to predict in advance.
- *Social/Socio-cultural.* Societies are constantly changing, albeit usually at an imperceptibly slow pace. Social norms develop, what was previously unacceptable or even unthinkable becomes commonplace, and old values seem to be left behind. However, values are notoriously hard to change, especially deep-seated cultural characteristics that have existed for generations. And yet revolutions do occur and have done so relatively recently. Businesses that have a strong social component may be vulnerable to such rapid changes in the socio-cultural environment, leading to unexpected increases in risk exposure.
- *Technological.* Most organizations are exposed to technological risk these days, not just tech companies. The rise of new technologies such as big data, AI, or genomics is likely to present both threats and opportunities that could be significant to many outside the tech sector.

- *Uncertainty.* This factor is a catch-all that covers all the others, but it also addresses nonspecific sources of uncertainty, including emergent risk. Businesses need to be alert to the known-unknowns, of course, and these are tackled by traditional risk management. But unknown-unknowns require a different approach, especially unknown-but-unknowable-unknowns.
- *Volatility.* Many of the sources of uncertainty listed previously are exacerbated by volatility, which is the tendency of a variable to exhibit large fluctuations in value. This is usually recognized in areas such as Economics or Market, but it can equally affect others. Volatility is often seen as a short-term issue, since things tend to even out over the longer term. However, even this is no longer true in some areas, as typified by the warning to investors "Past performance is no guarantee of future performance." Volatility may occur with a longer cycle time, and it does not just affect the short term.

Not all of these sources of uncertainty are relevant to every business, but each organization will be affected by at least some of them. The specific subset depends on the nature of the business, the industry sector, regulatory environment, size, degree of innovation, transnational reach, organizational maturity, competitive pressures, and so on.

We'll introduce the "risk radar" in Chapter 5 and explain how it can be tuned to the specific areas of interest for a particular business. But for now, it's enough to say that business leaders should identify those aspects of the external environment that are relevant to their organization, using Figure 2.2 as a prompt list. When the relevant subset of factors is known, the business needs to work out how to monitor each one, looking for signs of a developing Risk Hurricane. In the same way that meteorologists can track the precursors of a natural hurricane, business leaders must be aware of the external environment in which they operate, understanding the sources of risk exposure for their business, and looking out for concentrations of increasing uncertainty that could lead to major disruption.

INTERNAL ENVIRONMENT

The uncertain external business environment bears some resemblance to the warm ocean water, providing the context within which the Risk Hurricane can form. It is, however, not enough on its own—there's another important contributing factor. The first steps toward the development of a natural hurricane occur when the low pressure of a tropical depression meets warm ocean water. This low pressure corresponds to another factor in the development of the Risk Hurricane, which becomes potent when it interacts with an uncertain external business environment. That necessary other factor is the *internal environment of an organization.*

Internal environment is best reflected in *organizational culture,* which is defined as "the values, beliefs, knowledge and understanding shared by a group of people with a common purpose" (Institute of Risk Management, 2012).

The simplest model of culture is the A-B-C Model (Hillson, 2013), which recognizes that Culture is formed by repeated Behavior, and Behavior is shaped by Attitudes. A feedback loop is provided in the A-B-C Model, since Culture influences both Attitude and Behavior. This allows development of either a vicious cycle or a virtuous cycle, as the A-B-C loop becomes self-reinforcing. These relationships are shown in Figure 2.3.

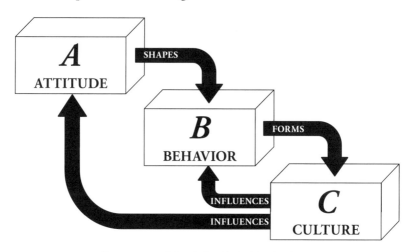

Figure 2.3: *The A-B-C Model of culture*
(From Hillson, 2013.)

For a Risk Hurricane to develop, one particular element of organizational culture is a key contributor, namely the prevailing *risk culture*. Drawing on the generic definition of culture, we can define organizational risk culture as "the values, beliefs, knowledge and understanding **about risk** shared within an organization" (Institute of Risk Management, 2012). The A-B-C Model can then be applied directly in the context of risk. Risk Culture is formed by the way we habitually and repeatedly behave toward risk, in our actions, decisions, processes, and reporting. Risk-related Behavior in turn is driven by our Risk Attitude and the way we think about risk more generally. There are also feedback loops in the risk version of the A-B-C Model. If we think inappropriately about risk, it will lead to ineffective risk-related behavior, and a negative risk culture will develop within the organization. Conversely, if we hold and maintain positive attitudes toward risk, it will produce effective risk management, building a risk culture that is strong, positive, and mature.

The basic links in the A-B-C Model are, of course, only a simplification, and more detailed models of risk culture have been developed. Notable among these is the Risk Culture Aspects Model developed by the Institute for Risk Management (Institute of Risk Management, 2012). This identifies eight aspects of risk culture, grouped into four themes, which are key indicators of the existing risk culture in an organization (see Table 2.1).

It's possible to use the Risk Culture Aspects Model as a diagnostic framework against which to assess the strength of the overall risk culture of an organization. This can be done either using a simple self-assessment questionnaire or through structured interview and audit techniques. These will expose specific areas of strength and weakness in the existing risk culture, allowing a targeted cultural improvement program to be designed and implemented.

The following questions will help you as a business leader to determine the maturity of your risk culture:

1. What tone do we set from the top? Are we providing consistent, coherent, sustained, and visible leadership in terms of how we expect our people to behave and respond when dealing with risk?

Table 2.1: Risk Culture Aspects Model
(adapted from Institute of Risk Management, 2012)

Theme	Aspect
Tone at the top	Risk leadership, clarity of direction
	How organization responds to bad news
Governance	Clear accountability for managing risk
	Transparency and timeliness of risk information
Decision-making	Well-informed risk decisions
	Reward appropriate risk taking through performance management
Competency	Status, resourcing, and empowerment of risk function
	Embedding of risk skills across organization

2. How do we establish and maintain sufficiently clear account-abilities for those managing risks and hold them to their accountabilities?

3. What risks do our current corporate and project culture create for the organization, and what risk culture is needed to ensure achievement of our corporate and project goals?

4. Do we acknowledge and live our stated values when addressing and resolving risk dilemmas? Do we regularly discuss risk dilemmas in value terms and does it influence our decisions?

5. How do our structure, processes, and reward systems support or detract from development of our desired risk culture?

6. How do we actively seek out information on risk events and near misses and ensure key lessons are learned? Do we have sufficient organizational humility to look at ourselves from the perspective of stakeholders and not just assume we're getting it right?

7. How do we respond to whistle-blowers and others raising genuine concerns?

8. How do we reward and encourage appropriate risk-taking behaviors and challenge unbalanced risk behaviors (either overly risk-averse or risk-seeking)?

9. How do we satisfy ourselves that new joiners will quickly absorb our desired cultural values and that established staff continue to demonstrate attitudes and behaviors consistent with our expectations?
10. How do we support learning and development associated with raising awareness and competence in managing risk at all levels?

By asking and answering these questions honestly, you can determine the maturity of your organization's risk culture and identify areas of weakness where the current risk culture must be challenged and changed. These can then be pursued by actively managing risk attitudes to change risk behavior and build a new risk culture.

Another way to test risk culture is to examine the risk mindset within a business. This outlines in more detail the "values, beliefs, knowledge, and understanding about risk" of an organization with a mature risk culture. A positive risk mindset includes the following values (Hillson, 2019b; Hillson, n.d.):

- *Risk is natural*. Life itself is uncertain, and this translates into every type of human endeavor. The risk mindset accepts this reality and doesn't struggle to remove all risk from every situation.
- *Risk is manageable*. There is always something we can do in response to each risk. Avoid a victim mentality—we are not powerless as long as we can see risk in advance. The risk mindset always seeks to influence risk, either by tackling its occurrence or addressing its effect.
- *Not all risk is bad*. Some uncertainties can be unwelcome if they occur, causing delay, damage, or disruption. But other uncertainties would be helpful if they happened, resulting in reduced costs or time scales, or enhanced performance and reputation. The risk mindset remains alert to both threats and opportunities.
- *Risk matters*. Risk is always linked to objectives. If a risk happens, it will affect our ability to achieve one or more objectives,

for better or for worse. Every risk is important, although some are more important than others. The risk mindset is relentlessly focused on objectives.

- *My risk is my responsibility.* It's easy to think that someone else will address risks, and it's "not my job," especially at work. But where risk affects my objectives, I need to deal with it. The risk mindset takes responsibility for relevant risks.
- *Proactivity is essential.* We often adopt a "wait-and-see" attitude to risk, hoping that we might "get lucky," with bad things not happening and good things just turning up. The risk mindset rejects wishful thinking and unrealistic optimism, understanding that prompt action is often required.

You can use these risk mindset characteristics to test the maturity of your organization's risk culture. A weak risk culture corresponds to "low pressure," which makes your organization vulnerable to the effect of an uncertain external business environment in generating significant risk exposure for the business. Where the values listed previously don't describe the way your organization currently thinks about risk, or where risk-related behavior doesn't reflect them, you might implement some or all of the following steps:

- *Build new thinking habits.* Leaders at all levels of the business can be trained to think differently. Take one aspect of the risk mindset and work on it until it becomes natural. This might involve formal training, as well as the engagement of facilitators, coaches, or mentors to support staff in changing how you think and act.
- *Develop emotional intelligence.* All staff need to be aware of how they think, learn how to check their thinking regularly against the values in the risk mindset, and make reflexive adjustments whenever necessary.
- *Communicate clearly.* Develop and implement a wide-ranging communication strategy that tells everyone why risk mindset is important and explains its elements in simple terms.

- *Be intentional.* Take the organization on a journey from conscious incompetence through conscious competence to unconscious competence. Be deliberate and choose change.

Another small parallel with the development of the natural hurricane may be relevant here. The initial low-pressure area that forms a tropical wave is not static: it moves in a westward direction to a place where it encounters warm ocean water, generating the conditions that can eventually lead to a natural hurricane. Similarly, risk culture is usually changing—sometimes imperceptibly slowly and sometimes more rapidly. Just as the tropical wave must move westward if it is to develop further, when risk culture is moving in a specific unhelpful direction, the likelihood of developing a Risk Hurricane is higher. That direction represents an incremental weakening in the risk culture, where poor attitudes toward risk become entrenched, risk-related behavior becomes a tick-box exercise where risk is identified but not proactively managed, and the risk culture continues to spiral downward.

This is why you and your fellow business leaders should pay careful attention to your current risk culture, assessing its maturity in the way discussed previously. If this shows worrying signs of weakness, then the organization needs to embark on a risk culture improvement program. This is likely to take some time, as culture is notoriously difficult to change. However, the A-B-C Model provides a hint about where we might start on the journey of culture change.

Some organizations start with B, thinking that if they impose changes in risk-based behavior, then that will lead to changes in risk culture. So they change risk processes, implement new risk tools, impose new risk reporting requirements, have more risk meetings. . . . All these changes in risk-related behavior are mandated in an attempt to change the way we behave toward risk and therefore change the risk culture. But the A-B-C Model shows that risk-related behavior is driven by risk attitude. If the way we think toward risk remains unchanged, externally imposed changes to behavior are usually temporary at best. When the pressure to change is removed, behavior quickly reverts to how it was previously.

The most effective way to change risk-related behavior in a way that leads to a more positive risk culture is to start at A, changing risk attitudes to modify the way we think about risk and seeking to develop a positive risk mindset.

RATE OF CHANGE

As we've seen in Figure 2.1, when the low air pressure of a *tropical wave* meets warm ocean water, together they form a *tropical disturbance*. This in itself is quite unremarkable and does not draw attention to itself. Something else is needed if a mere tropical disturbance is to develop further into a *tropical depression* and then into a *tropical storm* and ultimately a fully fledged *hurricane*. In the case of the natural hurricane, this factor is high circulating winds with low levels of vertical wind shear. Wind shear is defined as the amount of change in wind direction or speed with increasing altitude. When wind shear is weak, the storms grow vertically, releasing the latent heat from condensation directly into the air above the storm and allowing it to develop in intensity.

We've seen that the interaction between the "low pressure" of a weak organizational risk culture and the "warm water" of an uncertain business environment gives rise to the conditions for development of a Risk Hurricane. Simply existing in an uncertain environment doesn't necessarily lead to development of extreme risk exposure that has an existential disruptive effect on the business. It's when a weak risk culture meets the context of significant and sustained uncertainty in the external environment that the business will start to get into trouble. Initially, this may just cause a disturbance in the smooth operation of the organization, and it may go no further than this. But just as the tropical disturbance needs the additional factor of high winds to develop further into a serious storm, there's a third precondition for a Risk Hurricane—high sustained levels of change.

We've all heard the saying "Constant change is here to stay," or something like it. This well-worn adage exists in a number of forms and it has been attributed to a wide range of speakers and thinkers, but it is nonetheless true. The only certainty in our world is change (and death and taxes, and risk!). What is less certain is the direction and speed of that change. It is commonly accepted that both the rate of change and the scope of change have increased in recent years, affecting such diverse areas as technology, society, communications, and possibly climate.

Change doesn't present a problem while the organization is able to cope with it, but as the rate of change increases, businesses can find it challenging to keep up. In previous times, when change occurred at a steady and predictable pace, most organizations were able to sustain a rate of learning that was higher than the rate of change. This enabled them to absorb change and continue functioning as before.

However, we're currently experiencing increasing rates of change that are approaching exponential. If your business maintains its previous way of working, responding passively, and hoping to absorb change within its current practices, it will soon fall behind, become irrelevant and outmoded, cease to be competitive, and ultimately fail. This is likely to create conditions that favor formation of a Risk Hurricane.

To avoid this outcome, your organization needs to respond proactively to change, increasing your ability to learn and adapt fast so that you can stay ahead of the curve.

Figure 2.4 illustrates this situation. While the rate of change (the *solid line*) remains steady and low, most organizations will cope. As the rate of change increases, businesses that fail to respond proactively will be overtaken by changes (the *dotted line* in Figure 2.4), leading them into Risk Hurricane territory. By contrast, organizations that can learn faster than the world is changing will remain ahead of the curve and avoid corporate crisis (the *dashed line* in Figure 2.4). The difference occurs at the crossover point, where the rate of change exceeds the rate of organizational learning.

Of course, Figure 2.4 is merely conceptual, and the precise shape of this plot will be different for every organization. This is because the rate of change in their specific business environment will differ, and also their current capacity to cope with change will be different. This means that the crossover point will occur at

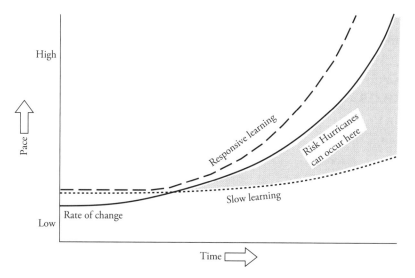

Figure 2.4: *Rate of change versus rate of learning*

a different place and time for every organization. Still, each organization needs to be aware of its capacity to cope with change, and business leaders also must be aware of the rate of change which they face. Failing to do so makes an organization vulnerable to an impending Risk Hurricane, where the effect of ever-increasing change can become catastrophic.

The other important point about Figure 2.4 is that the precise position of the crossover point is not fixed. You can take action to increase the capacity of your organization to cope with change. This can be done incrementally, or it can be done in more significant step changes, through such means as innovation, reviewing business processes, or, more radically, undertaking mergers and acquisitions, or entering or exiting a particular market. The *dotted line* in Figure 2.4 represents a *passive organization* that has a fixed capacity for coping with change which may increase slowly or not at all. The *dashed line* in Figure 2.4 indicates a *proactive organization* that is taking steps to improve its capacity in preparation for likely future change that hasn't arrived yet, allowing it to stay ahead of the change curve and delaying or avoiding the crossover into Risk Hurricane territory. This proactive capacity development might involve structural changes in the business to improve resilience. This is addressed in more detail in Chapter 6, where we discuss how to prepare for the possible arrival of a Risk Hurricane.

CASE STUDY:
GLOBAL FINANCIAL CRISIS (2007–2008)

In this chapter, we've described the three preconditions that lead to development of a Risk Hurricane: a *highly uncertain external environment*, *weak risk culture*, and *high rates of change*. A representative case study will help us to see how these combine together in practice.

The global financial crisis of 2007–2008 (GFC) has been widely studied as an example of unforeseen extreme risk exposure that led to major business disruption. We could use it throughout this book to illustrate many of the elements of a Risk Hurricane, but that would mean ignoring other instructive examples that offer valuable insights. Instead, we'll focus here on what led to the GFC, demonstrating how the three Risk Hurricane preconditions were at work.

The GFC was preceded by widespread lending at low interest rates by banks and other financial institutions in the United States to low-income customers wishing to purchase homes, in what became known as subprime mortgages. This had been encouraged by earlier legislation that encouraged lending to support affordable housing. New lenders entered the market with predatory low rates, targeting low-income ethnic minority customers, and the availability of cheap mortgages created a housing bubble in the United States, with around 20 percent of all mortgages in 2004 to 2006 being classified as subprime.

Financial institutions then packaged together these risky mortgages with other less risky assets, creating mortgage-backed securities and complex derivative products that were hard to monitor or regulate. Credit rating agencies assigned safe ratings to these assets, and they were sold to investors who were probably unaware of the level of risk they were taking.

The housing bubble burst in 2007, house prices began to fall, and mortgage rates went up. As a result, subprime customers started to default on their loans, and by August 2008 approximately 9 percent of all U.S. mortgages outstanding were either delinquent or in fore-closure. The value of mortgage-backed securities and related deriva-tives collapsed, leading to severe losses for financial institutions worldwide and a subsequent international banking crisis. The im-pact was much broader than the finance sector, of course, sparking a global recession that was the most severe since the Great Depres-sion of the 1930s, with massive government bailouts to prevent col-lapse of the global banking system.

Much more could be (and has been) said about the causes and consequences of the GFC. There is no doubt that it qualifies as a Risk Hurricane! In the context of this chapter, however, we can see with hindsight the existence of the preconditions that led to the for-mation of the GFC.

Uncertain External Environment

Several of the factors in Figure 2.2 contributed to a highly uncer-tain external environment within which the GFC took shape. These include the following:

- *Ambiguity.* The use of mortgage-backed securities (MBS), col-lateralized debt obligations (CDO), and credit default swaps (CDS) masked the true level of risk involved in subprime mort-gages, making these assets appear to be safe for investors.
- *Complexity.* The bundling of securitized assets introduced a de-gree of complexity that made it virtually impossible to track their actual level of risk exposure.
- *Ethics.* The presence of predatory lenders in the subprime mar-ket was driven by unethical practices, exploiting the desire of low-income customers to benefit from the housing bubble.
- *Regulatory.* Earlier deregulation of financial markets in the United States was a contributory factor to the GFC, allowing self-regulation of the derivatives market, and relaxing the net capital rule, enabling investment banks to substantially increase the level of debt they were taking on.

Weak Risk Culture

At the heart of the GFC was a misunderstanding of the true level of risk exposure. This was made possible by the prevailing risk culture of the time, which viewed risk pricing merely as a technical function. The possibility of falling house prices and the consequential risk of default associated with subprime mortgages were underestimated at all points in the investment chain, and there was no awareness of the aggregate risk associated with securitization of mortgage-backed assets.

None of the characteristics of a strong risk culture shown in Table 2.1 were evident in the leadership of banks and other financial institutions, with risk appearing to be absent from strategic discussions and decisions. A stronger risk culture would have set clear risk thresholds for the organization, with corresponding accountabilities and timely risk reporting.

High Rates of Change

Once the housing bubble burst and borrowers started to default on their loans, the situation unraveled very quickly. Government, regulators, and financial institutions were all taken by surprise and were making crisis decisions in panic mode in an attempt to impose some control and order. It's clear with hindsight that all the key players were operating in the gray zone of Figure 2.4, with the speed of their responses being some way behind the rate at which the situation was changing. Decision-making was overtaken by events, leading to suboptimal decisions and outcomes.

CLOSING CONSIDERATIONS

Now we know the preconditions for forming a Risk Hurricane. Armed with this knowledge, business leaders should consider the following actions:

1. Take the temperature of your external business environment, looking out for "hotspots of uncertainty" in the surrounding waters. Review the sources of uncertainty in Figure 2.2, determine which ones are hottest for your organization, then find

the ones to which you're most vulnerable and that you need to monitor most closely.

2. Test the internal environment of your business by assessing organizational risk culture. Be on the lookout for signs of "low pressure," with a weak risk culture indicated by the absence of a mature risk mindset and ineffective risk-related behavior. Determine which aspects of the risk mindset require urgent attention, and take immediate steps to strengthen them.

3. Monitor the rate of change around you. Change is often not easy to influence, but we can and must be aware of it, so that we are well placed to weather the "winds of change."

Clearly the one precondition for a Risk Hurricane over which we have most control is our organizational risk culture, and this is where we should pay particular attention. A strong and mature risk culture will mean that even if the external business environment is highly uncertain and the winds of change are gathering pace, our organization will be well placed to avoid the development of a full-scale Risk Hurricane.

THREE

Potency

All hurricanes are catastrophic, but some are more catastrophic than others. This may sound glib to anyone who has experienced a real hurricane firsthand, up close and personal. But interested on-lookers will be familiar with the use of categories to refer to the severity of a hurricane. This is particularly popular with the media in the United States and elsewhere, where hurricanes are tracked with some enthusiasm, using categories to emphasize their message. Sadly, there's a tendency to use "category inflation" to increase the impact of the news story, with the potential severity of an incoming storm being overstated to provide a sensationalist angle. Many of us have heard consecutive media reports over a period of a few days something like this:

> Initial bulletin: "Hurricane Anon is currently out in the ocean, bearing down on the mainland at high speed. At present it's a strong Category 3 hurricane, and it's expected to arrive in a couple of days, making landfall as a powerful Category 5. Mandatory evacuation will likely be imposed as considerable devastation is expected, with possible loss of life. This is not a drill; urgent action is required. A state of emergency could be declared at any time, and the National Guard are on standby."
> Next bulletin: "Get ready. Hurricane Anon is rapidly approaching our shores, strengthening all the time as it comes. Anon

currently remains at Category 3, but it has the potential to be-come a full-fledged Category 5. This could be the Big One, the most dangerous storm since Hurricane Horrible 50 years ago. Residents are urged to take immediate action; time is running out."

Final bulletin: "Hurricane Anon finally made landfall this morning as a Category 2 hurricane. While there was some initial disruption, the hurricane is expected to blow itself out over the next couple of hours, being downgraded to a tropical storm as it moves off into the ocean, where it won't trouble us any further."

The prominent (and often apparently unjustified) use of categories by the media emphasizes the fact that not all hurricanes are equal. But what are these categories, where do they come from, and what do they mean? And in the context of our analogy, are there also categories of Risk Hurricane, and how might they be defined or described? This chapter provides answers, explaining how to de-velop a Risk Hurricane Severity Scale that defines meaningful cat-egories of Risk Hurricane for your organization.

CATEGORIES OF NATURAL HURRICANE

A hurricane is defined as a Force 12 storm in the Beaufort scale (see Table 1.1), which describes it in terms of wind speed and wave height. For convenience, Table 3.1 reproduces the full hurricane entry from the Beaufort Wind Force Scale.

Table 3.1: Hurricane definition in Beaufort Wind Force Scale

Beaufort scale, description	Force 12, Hurricane
Wind speed	≥ 118 km/h ≥ 73 mph ≥ 64 knots ≥ 32.6 m/s
Wave height	≥ 14 meters ≥ 46 feet
Sea conditions	Huge waves. Sea is completely white with foam and spray. Air is filled with driving spray, greatly reducing visibility.
Land conditions	Devastation

This definition makes frequent use of the "greater-than-or-equal-to" sign (≥), clearly defining the boundary above which a storm can properly be called a hurricane. But this introduces a level of imprecision into the definition. For example, 75 mph is "≥ 73 mph," but so is 150 mph, and the two are very different, although they are both hurricanes according to the Beaufort scale. The use of the single word "devastation" to describe land conditions is also somewhat terse and uninformative.

Ever since the Beaufort scale was first made public, meteorologists have wanted to be able to describe different classes of hurricane. The accepted international definition of the Beaufort scale published by the World Meteorological Organization (WMO) in 2012 follows the original in having Force 12 as the highest level, but it also includes a set of widely accepted hurricane categories, based on work done in the mid-1970s by wind engineer Herb Saffir and meteorologist Bob Simpson. The Saffir-Simpson Hurricane Wind Scale (SSHWS) has five categories, based on sustained wind speed, as shown in Table 3.2.

Although Saffir-Simpson hurricane categories are formally defined only in terms of sustained wind speed, a brief indication of the expected level of damage is also provided as part of the SSHWS, as shown in Table 3.2. Initial versions of these high-level descriptors used only the headline generic terms ("some damage," "extensive damage," "devastating damage," "catastrophic damage"), which give an idea of the severity of impact that each category of hurricane might cause. Although this is a start, it is not very helpful in practice to people who might be affected by an impending hurricane. What exactly is meant by "extensive damage"? When does the effect cease to be merely "devastating" and instead become "catastrophic"?

To address this ambiguity, more complete descriptions of each category were provided by the US National Hurricane Center, as shown in Table 3.2. These have been further developed into the so-called *extended Saffir-Simpson scale*. This takes each generic phrase and expands it to describe the degrees of expected damage and injury affecting a range of specific areas, including people, livestock

Table 3.2: Saffir-Simpson Hurricane Wind Scale

Hurricane category	Sustained wind speed		Damage summary
Category 1	119–153 km/h	74–95 mph	*Very dangerous winds will produce some damage:* Well-constructed frame homes could have damage to roof, shingles, vinyl siding and gutters. Large branches of trees will snap and shallowly rooted trees may be toppled. Extensive damage to power lines and poles likely will result in power outages that could last a few to several days.
Category 2	154–177 km/h	96–110 mph	*Extremely dangerous winds will cause extensive damage:* Well-constructed frame homes could sustain major roof and siding damage. Many shallowly rooted trees will be snapped or uprooted and block numerous roads. Near-total power loss is expected with outages that could last from several days to weeks.
Category 3	178–208 km/h	111–129 mph	*Devastating damage will occur:* Well-built framed homes may incur major damage or removal of roof decking and gable ends. Many trees will be snapped or uprooted, blocking numerous roads. Electricity and water will be unavailable for several days to weeks after the storm passes.
Category 4	209–251 km/h	130–156 mph	*Catastrophic damage will occur:* Well-built framed homes can sustain severe damage with loss of most of the roof structure and/or some exterior walls. Most trees will be snapped or uprooted and power poles downed. Fallen trees and power poles will isolate residential areas. Power outages will last weeks to possibly months. Most of the area will be uninhabitable for weeks or months.
Category 5	≥ 252 km/h	≥ 157 mph	*Catastrophic damage will occur:* A high percentage of framed homes will be destroyed, with total roof failure and wall collapse. Fallen trees and power poles will isolate residential areas. Power outages will last for weeks to possibly months. Most of the area will be uninhabitable for weeks or months.

(From National Hurricane Center, n.d.b.)

and other animals, buildings of different types (mobile homes, frame homes, apartment blocks, industrial buildings, high-rise buildings), trees, fences, power, and water supplies. These scales provide more detailed indicators of likely damage, showing that the severity of the impact depends on the characteristics of the affected area. An example of these definitions of damage types is given in Table 3.3, which shows possible impacts from a Category 3 hurricane, providing a measurable interpretation of what is meant by the term "devastating damage."

Using the extended Saffir-Simpson scale, people and businesses in the path of a hurricane can see what type of damage they might expect, given the predicted hurricane category, allowing them to prepare appropriately. The goal is to enable appropriate responses to be taken in advance of the arrival of a hurricane. For example, if you live in an older mobile home that's close to some trees and you own a couple of horses and a Category 3 hurricane is forecast to move through your area, you need to evacuate your home and move the horses. Or if you own a high-rise industrial building, you can refer to the table of likely impacts and decide to reinforce your windows and move equipment away from vulnerable areas.

In this way, the extended Saffir-Simpson category descriptions are more useful to people than the formal definition in terms of wind speed ("Category 3 will bring sustained winds of 111–129 mph"), or even the high-level description ("Devastating damage will occur" from a Category 3 hurricane). People can simply review the headings in the extended impact table to determine which ones are relevant to their situation then check the detailed impact statements.

CATEGORIES OF RISK HURRICANE

Taking the lead from our analogy, it's possible to define different levels of risk exposure that cause business disruption. In the same way that the extent of likely damage against various criteria is used to specify Categories 1 through 5 of natural hurricane, so we can set up definitions of various classes of impact to determine the severity of a Risk Hurricane. We might even take the Saffir-Simpson

Table 3.3: Illustrative extended impacts from a Category 3 natural hurricane ("devastating damage")

People, livestock, and pets	Mobile homes	Frame homes	Apartments and industrial buildings	High-rise windows and glass	Signage, fences, and canopies	Trees	Power and water
There is a high risk of injury or death to people, livestock, and pets due to flying and falling debris.	Nearly all older (pre-1994) mobile homes will be destroyed.	Poorly constructed frame homes can be destroyed by the removal of the roof and exterior walls.	There will be a high percentage of roof covering and siding damage to apartment buildings and industrial buildings. Isolated structural damage to wood or steel framing can occur.	Numerous windows will be blown out of high-rise buildings resulting in falling glass, which will pose a threat for days to weeks after the storm.	Most commercial signage, fences, and canopies will be destroyed.	Many trees will be snapped or uprooted, blocking numerous roads.	Electricity and water will be unavailable for several days to a few weeks after the storm passes.
	The majority of newer mobile homes will sustain severe damage with potential for complete roof failure and wall collapse.	Unprotected windows will be broken by flying debris.	Complete failure of older metal buildings is possible, and older unreinforced masonry buildings can collapse.				
		Well-built frame homes can experience major damage involving the removal of roof decking and gable ends.					

(Extracted from https://www.nhc.noaa.gov/pdf/sshws_table.pdf, accessed December 30, 2021.)

Table 3.4: Risk Hurricane Severity Scale

Risk hurricane categories	Risk exposure	Impact summary
Category 1	20–50 percent chance of failing to meet one key strategic objective	Significant business disruption
Category 2	20–50 percent chance of failing to meet more than one key strategic objective	Major business disruption
Category 3	> 50 percent chance of failing to meet one or more key strategic objectives	Extreme business disruption
Category 4	> 50 percent chance of failing to meet all strategic objectives	Catastrophic business disruption
Category 5	Imminent business collapse	Existential business disruption

Hurricane Wind Scale (SSHWS) and produce an equivalent for Risk Hurricanes: the Risk Hurricane Severity Scale (RHSS).

At its simplest, this is a generic description of the severity of a Risk Hurricane, expressing degrees of "risk exposure that leads to business disruption." The Saffir-Simpson scale gives two types of information for each category: the wind speed and a summary statement of damage severity (see Table 3.2). In a similar way, the Risk Hurricane Severity Scale describes levels of risk exposure and a summary statement of the disruption to the business. Table 3.4 provides a generic set of categories of Risk Hurricane, with risk exposure expressed as the probability of failing to achieve key objectives, and simple terms to reflect the level of business disruption that would follow.

It's important to note that the Risk Hurricane categories in Table 3.4 are defined in terms of the impact on strategic objectives and the consequential disruption to the business. These factors are independent of the nature of the risk, so it doesn't matter whether your business is being affected by standard risk types that could be predicted in advance or by unpredictable types of emergent risk. The important thing to consider when trying to categorize a Risk Hurricane is to get a feel for how severe it might be, however that impact might arise.

While the high-level descriptors of impact in Table 3.4 have some value in telling business leaders what they might expect from different categories of Risk Hurricane, they don't help you decide what to do for your own organization. What precisely do you mean by the terms "significant," "major," "extreme," "catastrophic," and "existential"? It's clear that the meanings of these words will differ from one organization to another. More detail is required, putting flesh on the bare bones of these generic impact statements, similar to the way the extended Saffir-Simpson scale describes possible levels of damage in different situations (Table 3.3). To develop an extended Risk Hurricane Severity Scale, we first need to define specific and relevant impact types that are meaningful to the business and then expand the simple generic terms in Table 3.4 to determine the meanings of Categories 1 through 5 for each impact type.

In the same way that different types of effect are relevant to different groups of people for a natural hurricane, the specific impacts of a Risk Hurricane on an organization will differ between businesses of different sizes, industries, locations, and so on. As a result, it's not possible to provide a generic "extended Risk Hurricane Severity Scale" that applies to all types of business. We can, however, offer some guidelines on how such a set of impact types and definitions might be developed.

To do this, we need to go back to the simple definition of risk outlined in Chapter 1: risk is "uncertainty that matters." Different things matter to different organizations, and what matters is captured and expressed in their objectives. At the highest level, for the business as a whole, strategic objectives define the goals by which the organization will measure success, and they set the overall targets for the business to achieve. Strategic objectives are then decomposed into lower levels to produce a hierarchy of objectives, which explains in increasing detail what the various levels of the organization must do in order to deliver the overall strategic objectives.

We can therefore define the types of impact from a Risk Hurricane that are important to our organization by linking them to our strategic objectives. Then for each objective, we can interpret the five impact levels in the generic Risk Hurricane Severity Scale in

Table 3.4 ("significant," "major," "extreme," "catastrophic," "existential"). An example is shown in Table 3.5, taken from an organization in the energy sector that has implemented this approach. First, the business defined a set of seven specific impact types against which it wished to measure the effect of a Risk Hurricane (financial performance, project performance, operations, health and safety, environment, stakeholder relations, legal/compliance). Then for each category, five levels of impact were developed, presenting measurable criteria that the organization could use in practice. Table 3.5 shows an extract from the overall set of definitions for a Risk Hurricane, describing what this particular organization means by Category 1 "significant business disruption," Category 3 "extreme business disruption," and Category 5 "existential business disruption."

When you're developing these detailed impact scales for your organization, it's important to remember that the highest category of Risk Hurricane only occurs rarely (as is also true of natural hurricanes: only 4 percent of hurricanes since 1851 have been Category 5). If a Category 5 Risk Hurricane were ever to happen, the disruption would be existential (meaning that the business will cease trading), and the measurable criteria in the detailed impact scales must truly represent this. It can be hard to consider such conditions, even harder to write them down, but they reflect a severity of corporate crisis that you hope will never happen.

Once you've defined levels of impact against each strategic objective, you can then roll this out to different levels of the organization (functional, departmental, operational, project, etc.), creating tailored definitions of impact at each level that reflect the overall impact levels for the whole organization.

USING CATEGORIES

In the case of both natural hurricanes and Risk Hurricanes, the ability to label them using Categories 1 through 5 serves two purposes:

1. *Attention.* Despite the sensationalist tendencies of some media, it's helpful when communicating about an approaching natural hurricane to be able to distinguish between a relatively less

Table 3.5: Illustrative extended impacts for a Risk Hurricane (Categories 1, 3, and 5)

Category	Financial performance	Project performance	Operations	Health and safety	Environment	Stakeholder relations	Legal/compliance
Low (1)	< 0.5 percent change in core operating margin < 1 percent change in cash generation from operations < 0.25 percent change in working capital < 1 percent change in total asset base	< 1 percent variation in remaining project schedule < 1 percent variation in total project costs < 1 percent change in key project scope elements < 1 percent variation on project ROI	< 1 percent variation in production < 1 percent variation in productivity Loss of non-critical systems for < 1/2 day (without data loss)	Only minor injuries requiring first aid treatment	Only nonreportable environmental incidents	Local media attention lasting < 1 week No change in local community relations	No noncompliance directives No legal fines Zero civil liability
Medium (3)	1–2 percent change in core operating margin 2–5 percent change in cash generation from operations 0.5–1 percent change in working capital 2–5 percent change in total asset base	2–5 percent variation in remaining project schedule 2–5 percent variation in total project costs 2–5 percent change in key project scope elements 2–5 percent variation on project ROI	2–5 percent variation in production 2–5 percent variation in productivity Loss of critical systems for 1–2 days (without data loss)	Lost time injuries (LTI) with no irreversible loss of quality of life	Level 2 reportable environmental incident resulting in moderate environmental effect and/or short-term reversible ecological disturbance	National media attention lasting less than one week Local media attention lasting 1–2 weeks Temporary change (< 4 weeks) in local community relations	Temporary facility closure due to non-compliance Legal fines between $1–5M Potential civil liability

(continued)

Table 3.5 *(continued)*

Category	Financial performance	Project performance	Operations	Health and safety	Environment	Stakeholder relations	Legal/compliance
Very high (5)	> 5 percent change in core operating margin > 10 percent change in cash generation from operations > 2 percent change in working capital > 10 percent change in total asset base	> 10 percent variation in remaining project schedule > 10 percent variation in total project costs > 10 percent change in key project scope elements > 10 percent variation on project ROI	> 10 percent variation in production > 10 percent variation in productivity Loss of critical systems for > 5 days and/or irrecoverable data loss	Death or multiple permanent disabilities	Level 3 reportable environmental incident resulting in extreme environmental effect and/or irreversible ecological disturbance	International media attention lasting > 1 week National and local media attention lasting > 2 weeks Permanent change in local community relations	Permanent facility closure due to non-compliance Legal fines > $10M Unacceptable civil liability

severe Category 1 and a potentially catastrophic and life-threatening Category 5. Similarly, the existence of agreed severity scales can focus attention on an impending Risk Hurricane, making sure that business leaders, staff, and other stakeholders understand when something really bad may be about to happen.

2. *Action.* Just knowing that something is coming toward you doesn't necessarily help you to survive the oncoming storm. You need to turn attention into action if you're to make use of the information being provided to you. The extended Saffir-Simpson scale provides clear guidance to affected individuals and groups about what they might expect from a particular category of storm and what they should do to prepare and protect themselves and their property. Businesses facing a Risk Hurricane can also develop and use an extended Risk Hurricane Severity Scale to predict what impact might affect achievement of your strategic objectives, allowing you to take appropriate and proactive action in advance of the arrival of any expected disruption.

CASE STUDY: COVID-19 PANDEMIC

Let's look at an example of how categories of extreme disruption work in a real example.

Like the global financial crisis of 2007–2008 discussed in Chapter 2, the COVID-19 global pandemic was clearly a Risk Hurricane whose effects are still being felt across the globe. It's likely to become a standard case study in how to handle extreme risk exposure that leads to major disruption (or perhaps how not to handle it), and it could serve as a worked example for each chapter in this book. Here we focus on how we could have used agreed categories to understand and define the severity of the COVID-19 Risk Hurricane.

The disease known as COVID-19 is caused by a novel respiratory coronavirus that emerged in Wuhan City in China in late 2019. Early studies showed that it was a variant of the SARS coronavirus that caused Severe Acute Respiratory Syndrome in 2003, and the new virus was officially named SARS-CoV-2 by the World Health

Organization (WHO) in February 2020. Restrictions on public mobility ("lockdown") were introduced in Wuhan in an attempt to contain the spread of the virus, but by March 2020 the WHO had declared a global pandemic. By April 2020 over half the world's population was under some form of lockdown, with measures introduced to limit social mixing, use of facemasks to reduce person-to-person transmission, quarantining of infected persons, and tracing of their recent contacts. According to the WHO Coronavirus (COVID-19) Dashboard (World Health Organization, n.d.), by the end of 2021 over 270 million infections had been reported in over 200 countries worldwide, with over 5.3 million deaths attributed to COVID-19, making this the deadliest pandemic in recorded history.

Initial responses from national governments around the globe varied widely in the early days, with no consensus on the most effective approach. Some acted very quickly to introduce stringent measures, notably South Korea, where in February 2020, national mass screening and localized quarantines were implemented, infected individuals were isolated, and their contacts were traced and quarantined. International arrivals were also required to quarantine from April 2020, with a cellphone app to support mandatory self-reporting of symptoms. Current data in December 2021 (World Health Organization, n.d.) show that for total deaths due to COVID-19, South Korea ranks around 170 out of over 200 countries in proportion to its population.

By contrast, Brazil's government has been criticized for its slow response to the pandemic. In March 2020 President Bolsonaro condemned "media hysteria" about the novel coronavirus and declared, "For 90 percent of the population, this will be a little flu or nothing" (France24, n.d.). One year later, he was still opposing mask-wearing, casting doubt on vaccine effectiveness, and suggesting that the pandemic was "being used politically, not to defeat a virus, but to try to overthrow a president" (France24, n.d.). Brazil currently ranks eleventh in the world for deaths attributed to COVID-19.

One reason for this wide range of responses to the coronavirus pandemic in its early stages is that there was no agreed way of assessing its severity. Scientific data were still emerging, and expert opinion varied on the best approach to mitigation and treatment. When combined with very different political environments and styles, it's unsurprising that the responses of governments and their populations were so varied.

It would have been helpful if, early in the COVID-19 pandemic, a global body such as the WHO had defined severity categories for its possible impacts. National governments and others could have used these scales to assess how big this particular Risk Hurricane could be, allowing them to design and implement appropriate treatment strategies and monitor the effectiveness of these approaches in controlling the pandemic among their populations.

Earlier in this chapter we showed how to develop categories for business-related Risk Hurricanes, similar to Categories 1 through 5 for natural hurricanes. Table 3.4 gives high-level generic descriptors of increasing severity, expressed in terms of *the probability of failing to achieve key strategic objectives*, and *the level of business disruption that would follow*. It would be possible to adjust the nature of these two main scales to develop broad categories for a health emergency such as a pandemic, for example, defining *the likelihood of a population experiencing a given level of infections or deaths*, combined with *the effect on national well-being*.

However, the generic scales in Table 3.4 contain terms that are qualitative and ambiguous: significant, major, extreme, catastrophic, and existential. While these provide some sense of increasing severity and allow you to assess the likely category of a Risk Hurricane, to be properly useful it's necessary to expand these terms into more detail, as shown in Table 3.5. This uses measurable impact types that are linked to strategic objectives.

In the early days of the pandemic, initial assessments of COVID-19 risk by governments, their scientific advisers, and populations were broad-brush, using generic terms such as "critical" and "dangerous," or "trivial" and "minor." These vague expressions led to ambiguity, confusion, and lack of focus, as well as allowing people to adopt a range of varying interpretations of the same term. In the same way that the generic definitions of Table 3.4 are expanded into more detailed impact statements in Table 3.5, it would have been helpful for national governments to have access to an agreed-upon extended set of definitions of possible impacts of the pandemic against different areas of society, including physical health, mental well-being, health service capacity, economic performance, business viability, employment levels, supply chain reliability, community cohesion, and so on.

Each of these could then be expressed using quantifiable measures, such as:

- Number of infections per million of population
- Number of deaths per million of population
- Reproduction number (R), expressing how many people will get the virus from each infected person, on average
- Percentage hospital beds occupied by COVID-19 patients
- Percentage intensive care unit (ICU) capacity used by COVID-19 patients

If agreed severity scales for the COVID-19 pandemic had been published by WHO early on, there would be no confusion or debate over how severely a particular nation was affected. Subjectivity would be removed in favor of objective measurable data. But without an agreed-upon set of categories for the COVID-19 pandemic, based on defined and measurable levels of impact severity, different national governments had to make their own judgments of what they were facing and how they should respond. They were influenced by a complex web of perceptions and pressures and inevitably came up with a range of approaches, from aggressive to passive, and everything in between. It wasn't possible to have a sensible debate about the size or significance of the pandemic or to monitor and measure its waxing and waning, because there was no common language in place. Sadly, this situation remains unchanged at the time of writing, despite the emergence of new COVID-19 variants, where such a system of categorization would prove useful in assessing the associated risk to determine whether a new strain is a variant of interest or a variant of concern, and the extent to which we need to worry about it. Agreed-upon categories also simplify the task of communication with the public and allow changes in the level of risk exposure to be monitored as each wave of infection develops and passes.

CLOSING CONSIDERATIONS

Risk Hurricanes are not all the same; some are more potent than others. Different levels of natural hurricane can be described using recognized categories, and this chapter has shown how we can define categories of severity for Risk Hurricanes, both in general terms and using specific measurable impact scales. These categories are useful for focusing *attention* on the most severe potential sources of business disruption, as well as helping business leaders to understand what *action* might be appropriate.

Business leaders can take the following two steps to create specific severity categories for assessing potential Risk Hurricanes:

1. Clearly define strategic objectives, with measurable thresholds that reflect your organizational risk appetite.
2. For impact against each objective, determine what the following terms might mean for your organization: "significant," "major," "extreme," "catastrophic," "existential."

With these definitions in place, you'll be able to distinguish between levels of risk exposure that would cause significant disruption to your business and those that pose an existential threat, linked to an understanding of which strategic objectives are most likely to be affected. And when you know how potent an impending Risk Hurricane could be, you can then start to plan appropriate actions to prepare and protect your business in advance.

FOUR

People

Each natural hurricane has a wide range of interested parties who are affected in various ways. This chapter explores how different groups of people are involved in the occurrence of a hurricane. Following our analogy, we then reflect on the various stakeholders with an interest in a Risk Hurricane, looking at how and why they might be interested, and how they might be affected by a Risk Hurricane. In both cases, the perspective of each stakeholder group is determined by their position in relation to the hurricane (or Risk Hurricane).

PEOPLE INVOLVED IN A NATURAL HURRICANE

When a natural hurricane occurs, our thoughts turn first to those on the ground whose lives and property are directly impacted. There are, however, others outside the immediate zone of the hurricane itself whose involvement is more indirect. Finally, there are experts of various sorts with a professional interest in the hurricane. Before we consider what equivalents these groups might have for a Risk Hurricane, let's briefly remind ourselves of how each one relates to the natural hurricane.

Direct Impact

It seems right to start our examination of the people involved in a hurricane by considering those directly affected when the storm arrives. The degree of impact experienced by each group of people depends on their position in relation to the hurricane, so first we need to understand the structure of a natural hurricane, as illustrated in Figure 4.1.

A natural hurricane is a massive phenomenon whose dimensions are truly impressive. Typical hurricanes are about 300 miles wide (500 km), although the diameter of the storm clouds can reach up to 600 miles (almost 1000 km), with a height of up to 9 miles (15 km). At the center of the hurricane is an area of very low air pressure called "the eye," which is generally about 20 to 40 miles across. There are typically no clouds in the eye and the wind is calm. Around the outside of the eye is a wall of very heavy clouds with the highest sustained wind speeds, reaching up to 155 mph (250 km/h). The "eye wall" is the most dangerous part of the hurricane. Above ground outside the eye, there are large spiral bands of rain that can drop huge amounts of rainfall, causing flooding when the hurricane hits land. Wind speeds at the outer edges of the hurricane are lower than at the center, decreasing as the distance from the center increases.

We've noted that the level of impact experienced by individuals and groups within the hurricane zone depends on their position. Perhaps surprisingly, those within the eye of the storm experience the lowest level of direct impact, as this area is characterized by conditions of apparent stillness, with low air pressure, calm winds, and no clouds. As long as these people remain in the eye, they may appear to be unaffected.

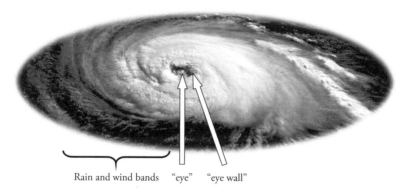

Rain and wind bands   "eye"   "eye wall"

Figure 4.1: *Structure of a natural hurricane*
(Public domain image from NOAA, n.d.)

Unfortunately for them, as the hurricane moves on, they will be exposed to the eye wall, where the danger is at its highest, due to extreme wind speeds and high levels of rainfall. The degree of damage felt by people on the edges of the storm depends on the distance from the center: the further they are from the eye, the more the impact decreases.

Indirect Effect

A wide range of other people are also involved when a hurricane occurs, in addition to those directly affected on the ground. These include the following:

- *Family members.* Relatives of those directly caught up in a hurricane experience a range of impacts, as they worry about the health and safety of their loved ones. Their anxiety and concern are often not helped by inaccurate and sensationalist reporting from the media.
- *Utilities.* The wider infrastructure outside the direct hurricane impact zone is often also affected, including power, water, transportation, and communication. As the hurricane causes inevitable disruption, utilities struggle to maintain services, exacerbating the problems experienced by those under the hurricane.
- *Emergency service providers.* First responders are called on to provide emergency assistance to those caught up directly in the path of a hurricane, including ambulance, fire, and police services. This may require acts of courage and heroism as professionals find themselves called into action to help others.
- *Media.* Both mainstream and social media have an important role to play in informing the wider watching world about what's going on, although reporting accuracy can vary considerably. This means that consumers of media outlets need to exercise vigilance and discernment when accessing hurricane news due to the apparently insatiable appetite for (melo)dramatic headlines and readership numbers, as well as likes and shares on social media.

Professional Interest

The final group of people involved when a natural hurricane occurs are the professionals. Their expertise gives them a unique perspective on what's happening, and it also enables them to offer unbiased advice and information to support those people who are involved either directly or indirectly. Two groups of professionals have a particularly important role:

- *Expert meteorologists.* These trusted and respected professional scientists have a key function in providing accurate and timely information to interested parties on the development and current status of a hurricane, as well as simulating and communicating possible future outcomes. They have access to powerful forecasting models, considerable amounts of historical data, and international networks of peers, all of which inform and shape their expert opinions. They also use a wide range of communication platforms to ensure that their message is heard, including mainstream and social media, websites, and emergency broadcast mechanisms. Their input is sought by national and local government, large and small corporations, transportation and infrastructure authorities, social and community organizations, and individuals, and the information they provide forms the basis of precautionary prior planning as well as immediate and post-event responses.
- *Global Monitoring Centres.* The World Meteorological Organization (WMO) maintains the World Weather Watch Programme (WMO, n.d.) to observe and exchange meteorological data, producing analyses, severe weather advisories and warnings, and related operational information. This program takes data from a network of Regional Specialized Meteorological Centres (RSMCs) and Tropical Cyclone Warning Centres (TCWCs), each covering a designated country or area, tasked with providing official warnings and information on severe weather, including hurricanes. For example, the U.S. National Hurricane Center (NHC) is the recognized RSMC responsible for tracking and predicting tropical weather systems in defined

areas of the northeast Pacific Ocean and the northern Atlantic Ocean. The NHC stated mission is "to save lives, mitigate property loss, and improve economic efficiency by issuing the best watches, warnings, forecasts, and analyses of hazardous tropical weather and by increasing understanding of these hazards" (National Hurricane Center, n.d.a).

PEOPLE INVOLVED IN A RISK HURRICANE

A wide variety of people and groups are affected when a natural hurricane occurs, and the type and level of impact depend on their position in relation to the center of the weather event. The same is true for the Risk Hurricane. A Risk Hurricane is defined as *circumstances of extreme risk exposure in business that lead to major disruption*. Many people will feel the effect of a developing corporate crisis, but the degree of impact from the resultant disruption will be different for each group.

Taking our cue from the people involved in a natural hurricane, we consider in the following sections who might be caught up in a Risk Hurricane, what the effect on them might be, and what actions they need to take. As for the natural hurricane, we look first at those directly impacted when a Risk Hurricane occurs, followed by consideration of the people where the effect is more indirect. Last, we turn to those with a professional interest in corporate crisis and disruptive extreme risk exposure.

DIRECT IMPACT—WITHIN THE EYE

When we consider people who are situated within the direct path of a Risk Hurricane, it's helpful to distinguish between the ones who find themselves in the eye of the storm and those who are further from the center.

The eye of a natural hurricane is a place of relative calm, with low wind speeds and air pressure. Similarly, when an organization is experiencing a Risk Hurricane, there is often a place of apparent calm and stillness at the center. This is where we find members of the board, the executive committee, and other senior business leaders. As the organization around them is being buffeted by the effects of extreme risk exposure, it's quite common for leaders to be shielded from the full force of the uncertainty. This may be due to the protection afforded by multiple reporting layers between them and the workplace, with information being filtered on its way up the hierarchy, and intermediate levels of management absorbing some of the pressure before it reaches the boardroom. It's also possible that they have only limited visibility of the intensity of impact being experienced by their colleagues further out from the center. Sitting at the top of the organization (perhaps within an executive ivory tower built on the apex of the corporate pyramid), they may survey the chaos and disruption below with a sense of detachment and objectivity.

This privileged position of relative calm for senior leaders can lead to one of two contrasting outcomes: *clear thinking* or *complacency*. The former is essential if the organization is to survive the Risk Hurricane, and the latter must be avoided at all costs. Important decisions must be made, often with limited time or information, and this requires decision-makers to be calm and unflustered. This can be difficult when the organization is in turmoil, when colleagues are stressed, and when normal business processes are failing to work as normal. But it is precisely at this point that clear thinking is most vital, and the position of senior decision-makers in the eye of the storm can provide much-needed respite from the worst effects of the Risk Hurricane while they consider their options.

If you are a senior leader, you and your leadership colleagues have two key responsibilities when your organization is experiencing extreme risk exposure from a Risk Hurricane:

1. *Protect and survive.* Your role is to take the strategic decisions that will preserve the integrity of the organization and enable it to survive the storm.
2. *Recover and thrive.* This means exploiting all the reserves of resilience that exist within and beyond the business, in order to support a robust and sustainable recovery.

To do this, you need information that will allow you to make good decisions under conditions of extreme uncertainty. Much of this information will come from within the organization. You'll be dependent on your colleagues and staff to provide accurate and current details in a timely manner. The information must tell you what you need to know that you don't currently know (attention) and what you need to do that you're not currently doing (action). This requires effective channels of communication to have been established well before the arrival of a Risk Hurricane. A full *information needs analysis* can define in advance what information is required by whom, who will produce it and from which sources, when and how it will be delivered, and how it will be used. This should form part of your corporate communications strategy, which covers how to communicate both in normal business circumstances and in times of crisis.

In addition to accurate and timely information, good decision-making in situations of high risk exposure requires a robust process that takes proper account of risk, and a degree of self-awareness and behavioral literacy that allows decision-makers to moderate their gut-level instinctive reactions with intelligence and intentionality. An approach to making this type of risky and important decision is outlined in Figure 4.2.

The process summarized in Figure 4.2 shows that before you can make a risky and important decision, you need to understand the decision context (which includes both the decision information and the decision-makers). You also need to estimate the level of risk associated with each decision option, which is driven by your (possibly unreliable and biased) risk perception. Finally, you need to understand your risk appetite, expressed in measurable risk thresholds, which must lie within the overall risk capacity of your organization. Armed with this information, you can then choose a decision option that lies within the approved risk thresholds. If no decision option falls within risk thresholds, it's possible to intentionally adopt a different risk attitude and modify thresholds accordingly, allowing a compliant decision option to be chosen. (Further details of making risky and important decisions are covered in Murray-Webster & Hillson, 2021.)

It's easy to say that senior leaders need accurate and timely information in order to make the strategic decisions that are necessary to

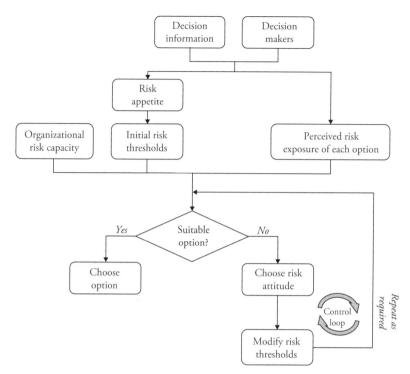

Figure 4.2: *Making a risky and important decision*
(Adapted from Murray-Webster & Hillson, 2021. Used with permission.)

cope with the arrival of a Risk Hurricane. And it's (relatively) easy to draw a flow diagram such as Figure 4.2 outlining a process for making decisions under conditions of extreme uncertainty. But how do business leaders get such information, and where can you find help with running the decision-making process? This calls for someone who is responsible for supporting strategic management of risk at the corporate level, who can gather and provide risk information and facilitate risky decision-making.

In some large organizations, this role may be filled by a dedicated senior executive called the Chief Risk Officer (CRO). Alternatively, it might be part of the responsibility of the Chief Financial Officer (CFO) or Finance Director (FD), or possibly the Chief Operating Officer (COO) or Company Secretary. Other businesses may look to someone who sits outside the executive suite, such as the chair of a Risk & Audit Committee, perhaps a Head of Enterprise Risk

Management (ERM), or someone leading a Governance, Risk & Compliance (GRC) function. If you fulfill a role like this, you'll know how important it is to gather risk information that supports robust decision-making and then to communicate it promptly and effectively to decision-makers, especially during the type of corporate crisis that a Risk Hurricane represents. You may also be called on to facilitate the decision-making process to ensure objectivity and counter bias where possible.

If you're a leader in an organization that doesn't currently have this type of risk-related role, you'll need to consider how to obtain the information you'll need to support you in making crucial decisions. Remember that during an active Risk Hurricane, your colleagues beyond the eye of the storm will be coping with the impact of extreme risk exposure, and they may not be in a position to respond to requests for risk information if communication channels have not been established in advance.

DIRECT IMPACT—AT THE WALL

Moving out from the eye of the storm, we first encounter the "eye wall," which is the place of maximum danger, beyond which lie rain bands and circulating winds. In a natural hurricane, the intensity of the rain and the speed of winds decrease as we move further from the center toward the outer edges, and the severity of impact similarly reduces, being proportional to the distance from the eye. For the organization in crisis, the level of disruption experienced by staff is also dependent on how far they are from the center.

The eye of a Risk Hurricane is a place of relative calm, with low pressure and rate of change. By contrast, the eye wall is the most dangerous part of the Risk Hurricane. Just as for the natural hurricane, where both the highest sustained wind speeds and the most intense rainfall occur at the wall, those closest to the center of the organization but outside the eye will be most affected.

This is where we find upper management and senior directors who report directly to the board and executive committee. They include functional leaders, departmental heads, regional directors, and operational leaders; staff with senior responsibility and accountability for significant aspects of the overall business. If this is your role in the organization, you have much to fear from a Risk Hurricane. You will be under maximum pressure, sitting as you do between the most senior leaders and the rest of the business. The bosses will be demanding accurate and timely information from you about what's happening across the organization. At the same time your colleagues and staff will be looking to you for leadership and advice to help them cope with the disruptive effects of the corporate crisis as it impinges on their own areas of work. You can easily end up being squeezed hard from above and below, as colleagues on both sides look to you for support.

If you find yourself at the eye wall of a Risk Hurricane, you'll need to draw on all the reserves of resilience at your disposal, including personal, professional, and corporate. Each of these resources will of course need to be in place before they're required so that they are ready to support and sustain you when the corporate crisis hits. This is when you'll reap the benefits of proactive preparation in times of relative calm, before any hint of an approaching storm arises. (We'll address preparedness and resilience in more detail in Chapter 6.)

DIRECT IMPACT—BEYOND THE WALL

Everyone in an organization that's in corporate crisis will feel the effect to some degree or other. But their experience of disruption will vary considerably, depending on their position in the business. For people caught up in a natural hurricane, impact decreases with distance from the center, and the same is true for the Risk Hurricane.

In general terms, we can track this variation across the corporate hierarchy, with the highest levels of effect being felt at the top, and only minor disruption at the lower reaches. Indeed, for many organizations in the throes of corporate crisis, it's common for senior leaders and managers to be losing sleep and working hard to contain the damage, while staff at the operational/functional workface or working on projects and programs may only experience minor bumps along the way, blissfully unaware that their bosses may be fighting for the survival of the business.

Although "distance" is most obviously measured by the number of levels of corporate hierarchy between you and the top, another factor is equally important in determining the degree of impact felt by different staff members when a Risk Hurricane strikes. We might label hierarchical distance as *proximity*, where high proximity means that my position in the organization is close to the top. An equally powerful driver of impact is *propinquity*, a related but distinct form of closeness. Where proximity equates to closeness in space, propinquity measures it in terms of how much something matters. High propinquity means that I am personally interested and involved in something and that I would therefore feel significantly affected by any change, either positive or negative. I might describe this as "skin in the game," though it doesn't necessarily refer only to financial investment. Propinquity might arise from my personal identification with the corporate mission or from the importance I attach to my career or professional status. I may be pressured by my family to do well at work, or my sense of propinquity might be driven by values such as altruism or a strong work ethic. Given the distinct nature of proximity and propinquity, they are not always correlated. In other words, it's possible for a staff member with low proximity (many levels below the top of the business) to experience high propinquity (disruption is keenly felt because the organization and their role in it matters a great deal to them). Similarly, a boss at the top (high proximity) may not feel too bothered by a corporate crisis (low propinquity) if they have other sources of income or means of support, so the disruption may not affect them significantly.

In the same way that the impact and disruption experienced by any particular member or group of staff is directly proportional to their proximity (hierarchical distance from the top of the organization), it is also influenced by propinquity (how much the business matters to them). This means that it's not always immediately apparent who within our organization is likely to be most affected by a Risk Hurricane. This is important when it comes to protecting and supporting members of staff during corporate crisis, as the levels of felt impact may be substantially different from what we might predict from their hierarchical position in the business alone.

INDIRECT EFFECT

While attention and concern naturally turn first to those people within an organization who are directly affected by the arrival of a Risk Hurricane, many others can also feel the effects. We listed those groups who can be influenced or interested when a natural hurricane occurs, and each of these has a counterpart in the case of a Risk Hurricane.

Family Members

We can use this term to describe other organizations that are related to the business that is being hit by a Risk Hurricane. It covers members of the broader stakeholder network, including clients and customers, shareholders, regulators, government, the general public, competitors, market analysts, and so on. It might also include other members of a corporate group, if the entity is part of a conglomerate. The degree of impact felt by members of this "wider family" of stakeholders will be driven by both proximity and propinquity, as discussed previously, reflecting the stake they have in the affected business. In the same way that relatives of those directly caught up in a hurricane worry about the health and safety of their loved ones, stakeholders of a business undergoing a Risk Hurricane can experience high levels of anxiety driven by concern about the ongoing viability of the affected business, but they'll also be worried about the extent to which their own interests might be adversely affected.

Utilities

This category covers those who provide essential services to the organization, notably members of the supply chain. In the same way that damage to infrastructure from a natural hurricane can affect people some distance from the epicenter, so the disruption from a corporate crisis can ripple through the supply chain to affect businesses a long way off, perhaps in different industry sectors or other countries. In some cases, supply chain impacts can be more disruptive than the original crisis, as the ripple effect spreads outward from suppliers to other unrelated businesses. The interconnectedness of modern business exacerbates this propagating influence, sometimes producing unpredictable and unforeseen effects far from the original disruption. In addition to the impacts felt directly by suppliers to an affected business, there can be a knock-on effect as they struggle to maintain normal service levels.

Emergency Service Providers

When a Risk Hurricane strikes an organization, the first responders are often insurance providers, banks, and other financial institutions, who are called on to provide emergency assistance to the business in trouble. They may also include investors and shareholders, depending on the circumstances of the organization. The assistance from these providers often takes the form of short-term financial interventions that would not be considered under normal circumstances. Sometimes governments may get involved, especially if the organization is in a critical sector such as infrastructure, energy, defense, or communications. Assistance might also be provided by consultants specializing in business recovery. With this wide range of emergency services available, the business suffering from the effects of a Risk Hurricane must be careful not to accept offers of short-term help that might create longer-term problems when the immediate crisis is over, as it's quite possible for emergency interventions to have unintended consequences for the ongoing health of the business.

Media

As for natural hurricanes, both mainstream and social media play a pivotal role in informing the public about developments in a business that's experiencing corporate crisis. But the business media are prone to the same tendency for sensationalism and partial reporting as other elements of the media. As a result, organizations need to have robust media-handling and crisis communications strategies in place as part of their Business Continuity Plans, aiming to manage the story as far as possible while the crisis continues, and in its immediate aftermath.

PROFESSIONAL INTEREST

The final group of interested parties when a Risk Hurricane occurs are those who take a professional perspective. For the natural hurricane, this includes both expert meteorologists and Global Monitoring Centres. These each have their equivalents in the world of the Risk Hurricane.

Expert Risk Practitioners

The counterparts to trusted and respected professional meteorologists are the risk experts and analysts who can offer impartial and effective advice to those directly impacted by a Risk Hurricane. Whether they are external risk consultants or in-house risk specialists, these experts offer unique skills that enable them to understand the factors that give rise to corporate crisis and that help them to identify the key drivers of extreme risk exposure. Their expertise allows them to recommend effective and proven practical strategies for addressing uncertainty, enabling the organization to both survive and thrive, not only protecting value but even creating value in the midst of disruption.

Professional weather experts use sophisticated forecasting tools to predict how a hurricane might develop. Similarly, skilled risk practitioners know how to use powerful analytical tools to model the effects of uncertainty on the business, and to assess the effectiveness (or otherwise) of proposed response strategies. Their expert advice draws on historical data and experience from a wide range of similar and disparate situations. They know how to communicate effectively about risk, ensuring that the key messages are heard and understood by those who need to know and to act. Their input assists with precautionary prior planning as well as immediate and post-event responses.

If you hold a risk-related role in your organization, you'll be aware of what level of support you can offer to your senior colleagues. You should also know the value of risk information in shaping business-critical decisions, and you'll understand how important it is that business leaders take full account of risk as they deal with the immediate threats and opportunities that confront them. However, although you may be clear about how you can help in the midst of a full-blown Risk Hurricane, your colleagues may be so absorbed by the disruption of corporate crisis that they forget about what you can offer. In these circumstances, you need to take responsibility for communicating risk information proactively. Two risk communication principles are important if your vital message is to be heard, received, and understood by busy senior leaders:

- *Speak their language.* Communication requires information to be passed from one party to another, involving both transmit and receive processes. The passage of information is made easier where these processes require minimal translation. Like all specialist disciplines, risk experts use jargon and technical terms that are understood by their colleagues but may be incomprehensible to others. When you're communicating about risk to business leaders, such tech talk must be avoided (no mention of probabilities, criticality analysis, percentile confidence levels, or Bayes' theorem!). Instead, your risk advice should be expressed in terms familiar to your intended audience. For example, the impact of key risks should be related to board-level objectives.
- *Focus on required actions/decisions.* Risk communication has two primary goals: to tell people what they need to know that they don't currently know (attention); and to tell them what they need to do that they're not currently doing (action). When senior leaders are dealing with existential disruption arising from a Risk Hurricane, they need accurate information fast. They probably don't have the time, patience, or mental capacity to listen to the results of your detailed risk analyses and how these were obtained. They just need to know what you've discovered and what you recommend them to do. When you're delivering a risk briefing, keep it brief!

If you're a risk expert from outside the organization, you have another challenge if you want your message to be heard. In addition to ensuring clear risk communication, you need to build trust with the senior leaders whom you're advising. For people facing the prospect of a natural hurricane, whether business owners or the general public, the weather forecaster is a trusted professional who can be relied upon to tell the truth when it matters. By contrast, if the leaders of a business facing corporate crisis need to seek risk-based advice from outside the organization, they have to proceed carefully. Unfortunately, the ranks of external professional consultants include some whose sales pitch exceeds their ability to deliver. When choosing a risk consultant, you need to be assured that you'll be working with a trusted professional.

The *Risk Management Professionalism Manifesto* (Hillson, 2002) provides ten criteria that risk practitioners and their clients can use to determine whether the risk services being offered are "professional" or not (see Table 4.1). These criteria provide a checklist that senior leaders can use when seeking support from an external risk expert. Each principle should form the basis for a conversation between the organization and candidate risk consultants, with the aim of establishing trust through a shared understanding of each other's responsibilities, as well as agreeing ground rules to be applied in case of disagreement. Table 4.1 also includes a set of test questions that illustrate how each professionalism principle might be applied in practice.

Global Risk Bodies

The weather profession has established a global network of Regional Specialized Meteorological Centres under the auspices of the WMO, tasked with providing official information on severe weather. This network allows early warning that a natural hurricane might develop, as well as providing expert advice on how to protect and preserve life and property when a hurricane occurs.

There's little doubt that we need a "WMO for risk," an internationally recognized single global body that is responsible for monitoring developing risk exposure and predicting the potential for a Risk Hurricane to arise. It would also be helpful if such a global risk organization included a network of "regional monitoring centers," each providing advice relating to a defined industry sector.

Table 4.1: Risk management professionalism: principles and tests

Principle	Statement	Test Question
1. Scope	The scope of a risk management intervention is the responsibility of the client.* However, the risk management professional is responsible for providing advice regarding the likely effectiveness of the proposed scope of work. Risk management professionals must inform the client if they believe that the chosen scope will be ineffective in achieving the intended outcomes, regardless of the client's possible reaction.	If the risk management professional discovers a potential flaw in the agreed scope of the engagement in terms of meeting the stated objectives of the client, what should they do?
2. Context	Risk management professionals must be able to demonstrate understanding of the context in which they offer advice and explain the boundaries within which their advice is given.	If the risk management professional gives advice that the client thinks is not "industry best practice," how should the discrepancy be resolved?
3. Competence	Risk management professionals must be aware of and stay within the limits of their competence. If they encounter areas outside their competence, they will notify the client. They will also call for review where there is substantive doubt about their proposed advice.	If a particular risk area is very technical or specific to the client's business, how much should the risk management professional involve client staff?
4. Processes and tools	Risk management professionals take responsibility for the appropriateness and effectiveness of the processes and tools used by themselves or recommended to the client.	If the client has a preferred risk tool or process, but the risk management professional thinks these are not appropriate for this engagement, how should this be addressed?
5. Quality of advice	Risk management professionals take responsibility for the quality of their advice. The client must be informed of any limitations in the processes or tools used, together with possible consequences for the quality or reliability of advice offered.	If the risk management professional considers that their advice is robust but the client's business is highly sensitive to the accuracy of the advice, to what extent should they be concerned about that sensitivity?
6. Language	Risk management advice is likely to be ineffective if it is expressed in a language or framework foreign to its recipients, such as offering engineering risk advice to business managers. Risk management professionals will frame advice in the language and framework understood by its recipients.	If risk management advice has been misunderstood by client staff, to what extent should the risk management professional be held responsible?
7. Recommendations	Risk management professionals must ensure that recommendations are feasible, achievable, and justifiable within the context of the client's constraints and that they are communicated in an appropriate and timely manner.	If the risk management professional considers that client staff are not implementing recommendations effectively, what should the risk management professional do?

(continued)

Table 4.1 (continued)

Principle	Statement	Test Question
8. Conflict of interests	All advice and recommendations given by risk management professionals must have the explicit aim of managing risks to client objectives. Advice whose purpose is to defend or promote the interests of the professional, their business, or colleagues is inappropriate. Risk management professionals will protect the client's competitive and proprietary information at all times.	If a risk management professional discovers a risk response that might be useful or relevant on an unrelated assignment, should they ask the client's permission before using the information?
9. Inappropriate application	Where a client indicates that they intend to use risk management advice or risk assessment results for ends other than the management of risk, risk management professionals will point out the consequences of such uses.	If the client chooses to transfer risk to a delinquent supplier to force them out of business, what should the risk management professional do?
10. Other objectives	The client, their organization, and stakeholders have many interlocking sets of objectives: strategic, business, project, safety, operational, etc. Risk management professionals ensure that their advice relates to risks affecting those specific objectives for which they have been consulted, while taking into account the effect of risks on other objectives where they are aware of them.	If the client has concealed some of the implications of the analysis from the risk management professional because of strategic sensitivity, what should the client do if the risk management professional identifies risks relating to those sensitive areas?

(Adapted from Hillson, 2002.)

*Note: The term "client" is used throughout the table to denote the person or party who receives advice from a risk management professional.

The nearest risk equivalent to the WMO is the *Global Risks Practice,* which forms part of the *World Economic Forum* (WEF, n.d.). The Global Risks Practice is a public-private collaboration comprising commercial organizations, academic institutions, and an advisory board of distinguished expert members. The aim is to identify and analyze critical global risks and communicate these to stakeholders and the wider public. This is primarily achieved through publication of the annual *Global Risks Report* (World Economic Forum, 2022), which is based on the Global Risks Perception Survey, completed by over 650 members of the WEF's diverse leadership communities. In addition to the work of the Global Risks Advisory Board, WEF has recently established the *Global Future Council on Frontier Risks* in an effort to understand and mitigate future risks and to amplify weak signals of coming disruptions in the decades ahead. Finally, WEF has launched a *Chief Risk Officers' Community*, bringing together CROs from the private sector and major institutions to share their perceptions of global risk and proven methods of tackling it effectively.

The WEF *Global Risks Report* includes an assessment of risk proximity, with a "Global Risks Horizon" that lists risks across various time frames from short-term "clear and present dangers" (0–2 years), medium-term "knock-on effects" (3–5 years), and long-term "existential threats" (5–10 years). The "Global Risks Landscape" presents a prioritized map of risks ranked by likelihood and impact, in five risk categories: economic, environmental, geopolitical, societal, and technological. A "Global Risks Network" indicates causal relationships between risks, revealing key risk drivers. Following these graphical summary representations, detailed discussions of key themes are presented in a series of focused chapters.

Given the scope of its coverage and the depth of its analysis, the annual WEF *Global Risks Report* provides a firm basis for organizations across the world to scan the current horizon for conditions that might give rise to a Risk Hurricane in their area of business. Indeed, the abundance of information provided by the report can appear overwhelming to busy business leaders, which is where risk experts come in. In the same way that professional meteorologists take data from the WMO and feed it into their weather models to produce forecasts that inform their users, so risk management professionals will be able to apply relevant findings from each *Global Risks Report* to identify the early warning signals that a Risk Hurricane may be on its way. The average person in the street doesn't need to read reports from the WMO to know if they need an umbrella or sunscreen; they simply listen to the weather forecast. Similarly, senior business leaders need not be fully familiar with output from the WEF Global Risks Practice if they have reliable and trusted professional risk experts to interpret the data for them.

Another risk professional body deserves mention here as a potential source of valuable global risk information. The *International Risk Governance Council* (IRGC) describes itself as "an independent non-profit foundation that aims to improve the understanding and management of risks and opportunities by providing insight into systemic risks that have impacts on human health and safety, the environment, the economy and society at large" (IRGC, n.d.). Its mission includes anticipating major risk issues and providing policy advice for key decision-makers, drawing attention to ignored, neglected, and emerging issues using international scientific knowledge from both the public and private sector. This mission positions IRGC as a predictor of possible Risk Hurricanes as it scans the uncertain future and provides independent advice to policy-makers and decision-takers in both public and private sectors, as well as offering detailed information to risk practitioners. This advice comes in the form of various publications, including white papers, policy briefs, detailed reports, concept notes, and opinion pieces.

In addition to the WEF Global Risks Practice and the IRGC, useful information on the global risk environment can be obtained from other global bodies such as the United Nations (UN) and its various specialist organizations, the World Trade Organization (WTO), the International Monetary Fund (IMF), and the World Bank. While these organizations are not specifically focused on risk, they can provide important contextual information about conditions that might give rise to a Risk Hurricane.

Despite the existence of these global sources of risk information, there is no single global risk body that parallels the role of the World Meteorological Organization (WMO) for natural weather phenomena such as natural hurricanes. There is in fact no "WMO for risk," with an equivalent network of "regional specialized monitoring centers" providing official warnings of emerging Risk Hurricanes in particular areas. This absence of a single recognized global source of risk-related advisories and information makes it more important for businesses to have their own way of scanning the risk horizon, drawing on all available resources to ensure that they are not caught unawares by a Risk Hurricane. (We'll discuss how to predict Risk Hurricanes in the next chapter.)

CASE STUDY: POLLY PECK INTERNATIONAL
The following case study illustrates the differing effects a Risk Hurricane can have on the various people involved, both within an affected organization and beyond.

Polly Peck International (PPI) began in London in 1940 as a small British fashion house founded by a husband-and-wife team to sell her designer clothing. Things changed in 1980 when it was bought by an investment company headed by Turkish Cypriot entrepreneur Asil Nadir, who used it as a growth-by-acquisition vehicle to build a widely diversified portfolio of businesses, including a packaging company, resort hotels, mineral water bottling, textiles, electronics, and homeware. By 1989 PPI had become a holding company for a worldwide group of over 200 subsidiaries, with market capitalization of GBP £1.7 billion, net assets of £845 million, pretax profits of £160 million, and over 17,000 employees.

Despite this success, there were rumors of accounting irregularities, and the UK Serious Fraud Office (SFO) started an investigation in 1990. Initial concerns about insider trading proved unfounded, but the SFO found evidence of massive transfers of funds out of PPI and into its subsidiaries, authorized by Nadir, totaling about £150 million. PPI also had over £100 million in short-term debt, with other long-term loans. As the investigation continued, the board filed for voluntary administration in October 1990, and the company collapsed in 1991 with debts of £1.3 billion. PPI was placed in administration, and most of its assets and share capital were purchased in 1994 by a competitor.

Charges were brought against Nadir for 70 charges of false accounting and theft, which he denied, and while on bail in 1993, he fled from the UK to his home country of Northern Cyprus, where he remained until 2010. He then returned to the UK to clear his name, but he was subsequently jailed in 2012 for theft. Nadir served less than four years of a ten-year sentence before being transferred to Turkey in 2016, where he was released after just one day.

This chapter has looked at the effects of a Risk Hurricane on a wide range of people, which vary depending on their position in relation to the organization. The PPI scandal and collapse illustrate this variation quite clearly.

- **In the eye of the storm**. As chairman and CEO, Asil Nadir sat at the center of the organization as the crisis at PPI developed, in a position of relative calm. This was only made possible by his active role in the accounting fraud, since he was one of very few people who knew what was actually going on. As the storm raged around him, he alone had all the facts, understood the situation, and was able to make rational decisions on what course of action to take. Even after he was charged with criminal mismanagement, he retained sufficient initiative to be able to skip bail and flee the country. He took the decision to return to the UK on his own terms, setting conditions under which he would face justice. Throughout the entire episode, Nadir gave the impression of being in control of events, even when they weren't going in his favor.

- **At the eye wall**. The senior management team of PPI bore the brunt of the uncertainty as the scandal emerged. During the period of rapid growth, Nadir had remained firmly in control, able to make payments without board or other management approval, and delivering astonishing profits through a complex and opaque structure. Several PPI directors had been concerned about the financial structure of the organization but had been unable to obtain sufficient details to confirm their suspicions. In early 1990 PPI's financial stability and its ability to pay debts were called into question. The board confronted Nadir about money transfers to subsidiaries and banks in Northern Cyprus, and they asked him to return the funds, but he refused. At Nadir's trial, the prosecution told the jury that the PPI board had been thwarted at every turn when they tried to work out what he was doing. Despite this, board members were held accountable for the organization after the scandal was exposed. Within a very short period of time, they went from being senior leaders of a highly respected and successful global enterprise to presiding over the collapse and liquidation of the group, with a consequential effect on their professional reputation and standing.

- **Beyond the wall**. Unsurprisingly, employees of the many PPI companies suffered directly when the organization collapsed. Few details have emerged into the public domain about the impact on management and staff at subsidiaries, but many lost their jobs, pensions, and career prospects as a result.

- **Indirect effect**. The impact of the PPI scandal beyond the organization itself was very wide. Shares boomed in the period 1980 to 1990, but shareholders and investors lost funds as the share price fell dramatically; share trading was suspended and PPI defaulted on its loans. Creditors eventually received about 10 percent of the £550 million they were owed. Suppliers were impacted as businesses ceased trading, and competitors benefited from the withdrawal of PPI from several different markets. PPI's group auditors Stoy Hayward were fined £75,000 with £250,000 costs. One British government minister resigned due to his close links with Nadir. Perhaps the most substantial impact was in the regulatory arena, as PPI's collapse in 1990 was one of several corporate scandals that led to the reform of UK company law, resulting in the early versions of the UK Corporate Governance Code. This has ultimately affected all future companies that have listed on the London Stock Exchange. Current best practice includes separation of the roles of chairman and chief executive and an active, majority-independent board to oversee executives, neither of which were in place at PPI. Indeed, if your business is subject to corporate governance regulations, you're experiencing the outer reaches of the Polly Peck Risk Hurricane, still affecting people over 30 years later.

CLOSING CONSIDERATIONS

Many people feel the impact of a Risk Hurricane, not just those within the affected organization. But the degree of disruption experienced is different for each group of people. This chapter has reviewed the level of effect felt by business leaders who find themselves in the eye of the storm, as well as by senior management, risk specialists, and other stakeholders, both inside and outside the organization. Each has a particular role to play when a Risk Hurricane strikes, and we all need to know in advance what will be expected of us when the time comes. The actions of business leaders and risk management professionals are especially critical in situations of major business disruption.

If you're a senior leader, you must make key strategic decisions to ensure the survival of your business during a corporate crisis and its sustainable recovery when the Risk Hurricane has passed. This will require clear thinking in the midst of chaos. The following steps will help you to make risky and important decisions effectively:

1. Establish in advance the sources and channels of risk information that you'll need to support your decision-making. This may require you to commission an information needs analysis that specifically details how you'll respond in times of crisis.
2. Ensure that you understand the organizational risk capacity and that you've determined your corporate risk appetite against each strategic objective.

Risk specialists both within and outside the organization also have two particular responsibilities:

1. Review the output from global risk bodies such as the WEF and IRGC, looking for early warning signals that might indicate the emergence of a Risk Hurricane.
2. If and when a Risk Hurricane occurs, provide timely and accurate risk information to decision-makers, expressing this in suitable terms that enable good risk-based decisions.

When each stakeholder understands and performs their role effectively, the dangers posed by a Risk Hurricane can be tackled with confidence, giving your business the best chance of emerging from the crisis with minimal damage, ready to move forward with the challenges of reconstruction and renewal.

FIVE

Prediction

So far, we've developed a working definition of a Risk Hurricane in Chapter 1 ("The Risk Hurricane describes circumstances of extreme risk exposure in business that lead to major disruption"), and we've considered the conditions that must exist in order to give rise to one, including an uncertain external environment, a weak organizational risk culture, and a high and sustained rate of change (Chapter 2). Recognizing that not all Risk Hurricanes have the same intensity, we looked at ways of distinguishing them by the severity of their impact (Chapter 3), then we reviewed how various groups of people might be affected when a Risk Hurricane occurs (Chapter 4).

This is fine, but how do you know when a Risk Hurricane might be heading in your direction? Is it possible to work out the trajectory of a Risk Hurricane in advance, to give yourself time to prepare for what's coming? Are there any reliable predictive tools that we can use? This chapter introduces powerful analytical modeling approaches that can indicate an oncoming Risk Hurricane and tell you where it might go in future.

FORECASTING NATURAL HURRICANES

Professional meteorologists play a vital role in ensuring that all interested parties receive accurate and timely information on the development and progress of hurricanes. They are the primary source for people and businesses who need to know if they might be affected, and if so, when and how badly.

To fulfill this role, weather professionals use a variety of specialist tools and techniques, taking data from a wide range of monitoring stations and instruments on the ground, in the air and from space, and feeding these data into sophisticated analytical models using powerful computers to simulate possible future scenarios. Proper explanation of complex meteorological models is beyond the scope of this book, but two aspects of hurricane prediction are relevant to our interest in Risk Hurricanes:

- The central place of uncertainty in predicting natural hurricanes
- The importance of clearly communicating that uncertainty to those who need to know

Uncertainty in Prediction

The statistician George Box famously said, "Essentially, all models are wrong, but some are useful" (Box & Draper, 1987). This includes models used by meteorologists to forecast the future behavior of natural hurricanes.

In a lunchtime broadcast on October 15, 1987, British TV weatherman Michael Fish made a confident statement: "Earlier on today, apparently, a woman rang the BBC and said she'd heard that there was a hurricane on the way. Well, if you're watching, don't worry, there isn't; but having said that, actually, the weather will become very windy, but most of the strong winds, incidentally, will be down over Spain and across into France." Later that same evening and overnight, the so-called "Great Storm of 1987" arrived in southern England with winds of up to 115 mph, which left 1.4 million homes without power, felled 15 million trees, and killed 18 people. It was the most damaging storm to hit the UK since 1703, and insurance claims totaled over GBP £2 billion.

Despite the power of currently available hurricane forecasting models, they can never give precise results with 100% accuracy and

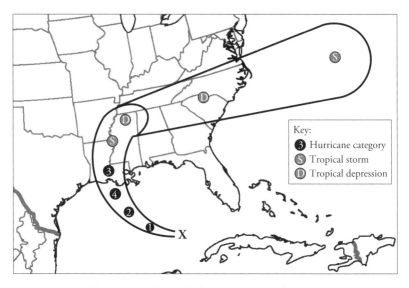

Figure 5.1: *Example hurricane track forecast*

certainty. This is because of the complex nature of the atmosphere, with multiple variables to be considered, including wind speed and direction, pressure, temperature, and moisture, at given locations and times. Meteorologists create a model of the current state of the atmosphere as the starting point for a forecast, but this inevitably differs from the real world, building uncertainty into subsequent forecasts.

It's important that users of forecasts understand the inbuilt uncertainty associated with hurricane forecasting. Anyone who has watched the Weather Channel on TV will be familiar with the way the professionals present the uncertainty that is inherent in forecasting the track of a natural hurricane. The primary tool for this is the "cone of uncertainty," as illustrated in Figure 5.1 (based on the forecast track for Hurricane Laura on August 25, 2020). This cone represents the probable area where forecasters expect the center of a storm to be at any given point in time, measured in 12-hour increments from the current time, based on historical data that gives 60 to 70 percent accuracy in prediction.

The cone starts with the current position of the center of the weather system (marked *X* in Figure 5.1) and shows where it might go in the coming hours and days. In the immediate future, the possible variations are small, with a narrow band of possible positions for the storm center. Very-short-term predictions are almost certain, but the degree of uncertainty becomes greater the further out the prediction goes, increasing with time, until we get to the extreme reaches of forecasting possibilities, where the range of positions that the storm might end up is too broad to be useful.

Along with the likely track of the storm, the forecast also predicts possible changes in its strength. It's common to start drawing attention to a weather system while it is still a tropical storm, before it gains hurricane status. As the prediction extends into the future, weather forecasters give an indication of when and where the tropical storm might become a hurricane, and they then predict its potential progression through Categories 1 to 5, and subsequent decline back down through the categories and into lower-intensity storm status. One important aspect of the forecast is the likely maximum category that this hurricane is expected to reach. Combining this with the predicted track allows people and businesses in the path of the storm to take protective measures in advance, knowing whether they could face significant disruption and damage.

Despite the level of detail presented by professional meteorologists in their public predictions, it's important to remember that the cone of uncertainty is only a *prediction* of the hurricane's possible position, and it is not a guarantee. The positional track and associated changes in storm strength are outputs from a sophisticated and complex model, based on many data sources, which involve differing degrees of uncertainty. As each day passes and estimates are replaced with hard facts, the model is refined and its outputs change. This leads to a revision in the position of the cone of uncertainty, which is reported in the weather forecasts. Such revisions don't mean that the previous forecast was wrong, merely that the forecasters now have more concrete information on which to base their predictions.

The accuracy of predictions is also being improved over time as the methodology is enhanced, with improved observations from observing stations and newly launched satellites, advances in oceanic and atmospheric research, more robust modeling, and more powerful supercomputing. As a result, users today can have improved confidence in current forecasts compared to what was previously available.

Despite these impressive developments in forecasting technology, the cone of uncertainty is an admission that there is a significant margin of error in all forecasts, and this margin increases the further the forecast reaches into the future. The fact that forecasts change with time can be confusing to people who rely on them to support crucial decisions on when and how to prepare and respond. This is why the task of communicating uncertainty is so vital.

Communicating Uncertain Predictions

Information about a developing hurricane is communicated via two main channels: mainstream media, including television, and local emergency management agencies or other local authorities.

- *Mainstream media.* The cone of uncertainty described previously is almost universally used by weather forecasters to describe hurricane track predictions, and it is widely recognized by the viewing public. But many people misunderstand what it can and can't be used for. The key misunderstanding is around the area covered by the cone of uncertainty. Many people are unaware that the cone only shows the predicted position of the storm center, and the full extent of the weather system extends well beyond the cone. It is commonly believed that storm impacts will only occur inside the cone and other areas are not at risk of strong winds or heavy rain. People and businesses located outside the cone may therefore feel an unjustified sense of relief or complacency.

  This type of common misunderstanding places a significant responsibility on those charged with communicating hurricane forecasts to the general public. Television weather presenters have developed a standard script to explain the cone of uncertainty, and this is repeated frequently during hurricane season to minimize the risk of misinterpretation. By using a simple visual representation (the cone of uncertainty) together with a repeated simple explanation, professional meteorologists aim to communicate essential information with minimal misunderstanding.

- *Local emergency management agencies.* Local authorities are responsible for issuing official warnings and instructions to residents and businesses, based on information received from professional meteorologists. This includes advice on when to start preparations for the possible arrival of a storm, with advance warning of the likely time, duration, and intensity of a hurricane, through to mandatory instructions to evacuate. Local authorities use two standard levels of alert, which are clearly defined, each associated with specific actions that must be taken when the alert is issued: a *hurricane watch* means that hurricane conditions are *possible* and people should get ready to take action; a *hurricane warning* means that a hurricane is *expected* and people should leave as soon as directed by local officials. Both types of communication are issued well before hurricane conditions arrive, to enable necessary preparations to be made before they become too difficult.

FORECASTING RISK HURRICANES

Professional meteorologists forecast the possible path and likely severity of a natural hurricane using sophisticated and powerful models, and they translate these into simple messages to communicate essential information to those who need to know. Risk specialists face the same two-fold challenge when a Risk Hurricane is on the horizon:

- How to analyze the likely behavior of an impending Risk Hurricane
- How to pass on useful and timely information about risk

Fortunately, our analogy provides several important insights to address these two aspects, starting with the sources of data about Risk Hurricanes. Weather forecasters gather atmospheric data from monitoring stations on land, on sea, and in space; in the same way, risk professionals have access to multiple rich sources of risk data.

These sources include mining relevant risk knowledge from previous experience, lessons-learned knowledge bases, industrial norms, and historical case studies. Where the organization has an enterprise-wide risk management (ERM) framework in place, this can be used to spot patterns of risk within and across the business, uncovering common causes of risk, identifying hotspots of risk exposure, or aggregating similar risks that arise in disparate locations or organizational units. The use of so-called "horizon-scanning" techniques (Institute of Risk Management, 2018) ensures that a wider perspective is taken, reviewing trend reports produced by official sources such as government agencies, international organizations, and global risk bodies (discussed in the previous chapter).

Complementing these various risk sources is the risk process itself, which is sometimes referred to as a "forward-looking risk radar," scanning the uncertain future to identify developing risks that may prove to be relevant. Like a real radar, the risk process is designed to spot uncertainties "at a distance" while they are way off in the future, providing early warning that a significant risk may be on its way. When such a risk is spotted in the future, its precise characteristics may not be clear, but this doesn't always matter. It can be enough for the "risk radar" to see a big bad thing developing, which appears to be heading toward us and might cause severe disruption. Of course, the "risk radar" may also spot a large and potentially beneficial opportunity developing on the horizon, which may be coming in our direction, offering significant advantages if we can exploit it.

The aim is to use the forward-looking nature of the "risk radar" to discern the potential size of a significant risk (risk quantification), as well as estimating its speed and direction of travel (risk velocity), so that we can give our senior decision-makers enough time to respond proactively. Where results indicate the possibility of a major disruptive event, the response of senior leaders may be to change our position so that the oncoming threat doesn't hit us directly (threat avoidance), to develop protective measures that would mitigate any potential negative impact (threat reduction), or enlist the help of others who may be able to deal effectively with the situation (threat transfer). Conversely, if a large opportunity is spotted, decision-makers may adjust our strategy to move us into its path and ensure that we capture the additional benefits that it offers (opportunity exploitation), take steps to maximize its beneficial impact (opportunity enhancement), or involve others in helping us to manage it (opportunity sharing).

Once we've gathered risk data, we're in a position to determine whether a Risk Hurricane might be developing in our future. Like meteorologists, risk practitioners have a range of powerful and sophisticated analytical models available. And like weather forecasters, we face the challenge of translating findings into actionable messages.

MODELING RISK

When risk specialists want to model the combined effect of multiple uncertainties and determine the range of possible outcomes, their thoughts turn naturally to probabilistic modeling using Monte Carlo simulation, with a range of techniques that are known collectively as quantitative risk analysis (QRA). These techniques are well known and have been in use for many years (Vose, 2008; Hulett, 2011), and they are supported by a wide range of software tools that offer reliable analysis based on established mathematical principles. Detailed description of QRA techniques is beyond our scope here, but a few key ideas are worth emphasizing:

- *Defined purpose.* We must understand why we need to do this analysis. What is its scope? For example, are we making a "go/no-go" strategic decision, working out how much contingency we need, or trying to find the biggest risks? We may only be interested in one type of risk exposure, such as risk to profitability, share price, market share, or cash flow. Or maybe we want an integrated view of the overall risk exposure that may result from this Risk Hurricane. The questions to be answered should be clearly defined at the start, and, since we are using quantitative methods, the objectives of our analysis must be quantifiable and measurable.

- *Robust foundation.* Einstein's advice to "Make things as simple as possible, but not simpler" is the key to a good risk model. It must reflect reality at a level that allows the effect of risk to be visible, and we should use a modeling approach and baseline that match the level of analysis that we are undertaking.

- **Best available data**. A risk model is only as good as the data it is fed. These must reflect all relevant risks, including both *threats* and *opportunities*. We must estimate possible *variability* on known parameters (using ranges of values), as well as reflecting areas of *ambiguity* and *alternative options* (using stochastic branches). We also need to identify *dependencies* between risks (using correlation).

- **Expose risk drivers**. The completed model must be validated before use to check that it is robust, with no data input errors or false logic, and any errors should be corrected before proceeding. The main drivers of risk exposure can then be revealed by running alternative versions of the risk model with key variables modified, and comparing the results.

- **Test responses**. We can also use the risk model to determine the likely effect of possible risk responses, by comparing the outcomes with and without action. This will show how different response options would affect the overall risk exposure and the degree to which they are adequate and effective.

- **Decide!** Risk models can tell us many useful things about risk exposure, including the range of possible outcomes, the likelihood of achieving our objectives and targets, the most influential risks, the main risk drivers, and the most effective actions. Now we need to decide what to do next! Actions could include anything from minor tactical adjustments to adopting a completely new strategy.

There are three distinct approaches to building risk models that form the basis for predicting the behavior of a Risk Hurricane:

1. The most commonly used method *starts with an existing baseline,* like a strategic plan or budget, then adds in specific risks and other sources of uncertainty. This shows the influence that individual risks or uncertainties might have on outcomes and

objectives, allowing us to identify and prioritize those that require our attention and action.

2. It's also possible to *model risks in isolation*, separate from a baseline plan, focusing on finding the worst threats and the best opportunities.

3. Alternatively, and less commonly, we can *represent the entire organization (or elements of it) as a system*, using simple influence diagrams or more complex system dynamics models, into which risks and uncertainties are added. Non-risk versions of these models should operate in steady-state conditions, but including risk and uncertainty will cause instability in the system, leading to unforeseen outcomes. These can arise from previously unidentified feedback or feedforward loops or from unrecognized dependencies and linkages within the system.

One key role of the risk specialist is to understand the capabilities and limitations of different types of risk model, and to know when each type is useful. They should also be able to build, run, and interpret risk models as required, or at least be an "intelligent customer" who can commission other risk experts to do the necessary risk modeling and then use the results appropriately. One key distinction between the three types of risk model outlined previously is the type of uncertainty for which they are typically used. The first two model types (adding risk and uncertainty to an existing baseline, or modeling risks in isolation) are useful when you wish to explore the range of outcomes that could arise from a set of known risks and uncertainties. These are the most common types of risk model used by risk specialists. But the extreme level of risk exposure associated with a Risk Hurricane is often the result of more than an accumulation of multiple known risks: instead, the conditions that cause a Risk Hurricane to arise usually include risks that were unforeseen, and perhaps even some that were unforeseeable. These types of risk are hard to incorporate into the standard modeling approaches, but they can be addressed using system-based modeling (Williams, 2002).

In system-based models, in addition to specific risks and other sources of uncertainty, it's possible to include causes and effects. This means we can model what might happen to our organization (the "system") if unforeseeable risks emerge from recognizable causes, or if currently unknown risks occur and impact us. The International Risk Governance Council (IRGC) published a ground-breaking report detailing twelve generic causes of emergent risk (International Risk Governance Council, 2010), including:

1. *Scientific unknowns.* Uncertainties within data or information may mean that emerging risks will be unanticipated, unnoticed, or under-/overestimated.
2. *Loss of safety margins.* Risks are more likely to emerge where there's tight coupling and connectivity of system components combined with pressure to reduce cycle time, with reduced slack or buffering capacity.
3. *Positive feedback.* Vicious cycles can arise within systems that destabilize and exacerbate the impact of change that emergent risks bring.
4. *Varying susceptibilities.* Different groups of people (stakeholders) are affected differently by emergent risks, and what's trivial to some may be existential to others.
5. *Conflicting interests.* Values and interests don't always overlap with scientific data, and conflict can lead to emerging risks being ignored or amplified.
6. *Social dynamics.* Underlying social change can generate or amplify emerging risks, and these factors are often not visible and/or not well understood.
7. *Technological advances.* When technological change is not carefully monitored or regulated, its effects can be unpredictable and unexpected.
8. *Temporal complications.* Time-based issues are common with emergent risks, for example, if there's a long delay between a risk's emergence and its visible effects.
9. *Inadequate communications.* Emergent risks can be caused, complicated, or amplified by untimely, incomplete, misleading, or absent communication.

10. *Information asymmetry.* Unexpected risks can arise when some stakeholders possess information that isn't available to others, intentionally or accidentally.

11. *Perverse incentives.* Emergent risk can be caused by motivators that induce counterproductive or undesirable behaviors or that lead to negative or unintended consequences.

12. *Malicious motives and acts.* The actions of those with malicious intent can produce risks that were not foreseen, exacerbated by global connectedness and shared infrastructure.

It's possible to tune your "forward-looking risk radar" to monitor these twelve generic causes, and where you spot one or more of them developing in your environment, they can be included in a system-based risk model. This allows you to explore the effects of emergent risks that you haven't yet identified, by linking their causes to elements of your organization.

It's also possible to take account of unforeseeable risks in a system-based risk model by reflecting their effects, even when the specific details of the risks themselves are not apparent. This approach was popularized by Nassim Nicholas Taleb in his book *The Black Swan: The Impact of the Highly Improbable* (Taleb, 2007), where he discussed the existence of risks that are not only currently unknown but that could never be known because they are beyond our current frame of reference. The term "Black Swan" is commonly used for risks that have extremely low probability of occurrence and extremely high impact, but Taleb's initial concept was different. He says that a true Black Swan has three characteristics:

1. *Unexpected and unpredictable outlier.* Black Swans are by nature inconceivable, since they lie totally outside our previous experience and could never be predicted based on our current understanding of the way the world works. This means that it's impossible to predict a Black Swan: it is literally an unknowable-unknown.

2. *Extreme impact.* When a Black Swan does occur, it has a huge effect, possibly made bigger by the fact that it's always totally unexpected. However, we should remember that not all Black Swans are bad; like all risks, they can have upside impacts as well as downside.

3. *Appears obvious after occurrence.* Despite being beyond our capacity to imagine before it occurs, after a Black Swan has happened it is commonly rationalized with the benefit of hindsight, and the consensus view is that we should have seen it coming.

Although specific Black Swan events are unpredictable, it is possible to consider the likely effects of an unknowable-unknown. This is common in business continuity planning, where the particulars of a disruptive event are less important than the nature of the disruption. We can start from the idea that "something significantly disruptive might happen" and then analyze the impact of that "something," whatever it might be. These types of generic effects from possible Black Swans can be included in a system-based risk model alongside generic causes of emergent risk and more traditional individual risks and uncertainties, allowing a comprehensive analysis that takes into account all types of risk. This approach offers a powerful way of predicting the possible path and severity of a Risk Hurricane, even where some of the contributing factors are not well defined.

COMMUNICATING RISK

Weather forecasters have developed simple ways of passing on the results of complex meteorological modeling, using standard format graphics like the "cone of uncertainty." Similar outputs are available for predicting the development of a Risk Hurricane.

The QRA models used by risk specialists to analyze uncertainty are based on Monte Carlo simulation. The standard outputs from this type of analysis are familiar to many, particularly the cumulative probability curve (usually called an "S-curve" due to its shape). The analysis calculates a range of possible values for an output variable and presents these as a cumulative distribution curve. This can be used to determine the degree of confidence associated with any particular value, allowing decision-makers to make risk-informed decisions that reflect their chosen risk appetite. Two examples of this type of S-curve are shown in Figure 5.2, analyzing possible outturn values for the completion date (Figure 5.2a) and cost (Figure 5.2b) associated with a merger project. The project plan suggested a completion date of June 1, and the QRA result indicates that the project

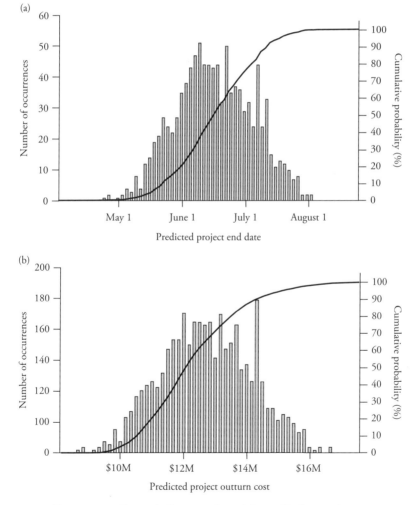

Figure 5.2: *Example S-curves from Monte Carlo simulation*

is expected to complete in mid-June (the weighted average of all individual simulation results, or "iterations"), with a possible range running from early May to late July. On average the project will cost just over $12 million, although it could be anywhere between $10 million to $16 million. Given this information, senior leaders can decide whether to proceed with the merger, and if so, what budget to allocate to the project.

For many (perhaps most) users of QRA techniques, this type of S-curve is the main (perhaps only) output that they produce to support risk-based decision-making. It's true that the standard S-curve is useful in indicating the range of possible outcomes that might result for a given parameter, given a baseline plan and a set of risks and uncertainties. But QRA offers a great deal more valuable information than what is available from S-curves. Those who regard themselves as more advanced might supplement S-curves with tornado plots, sensitivity charts, or criticality diagrams. But none of these typical QRA outputs help us to understand the possible future trajectory of a developing Risk Hurricane. This requires a different type of analytical output.

We've seen that the future path taken by a natural hurricane cannot be known with absolute certainty, so forecasters start with its current known position then present a range of alternative paths, as shown in Figure 5.1. As time passes, so the degree of uncertainty increases and variation in the possible path of the hurricane becomes wider. Senior leaders in an organization facing the possibility of major business disruption from a Risk Hurricane need similar time-based information. Given our current position and the uncertainties we can see on our "risk radar," how might the potential impact of the Risk Hurricane progress with time?

This requires information that the standard S-curve cannot provide. We need something that shows how uncertainty might vary with time. The key tool in communicating this type of prediction is an analytical output that is called a "football plot" in the United States, based on the shape of the graphic, which resembles the shape of the ball used in American football. (In other countries, where the game known as "football" is played with a spherical ball, this report format is called an "eyeball plot.") This output results from use of an integrated cost-schedule risk model, where both parameters are varied together during the Monte Carlo simulation. An example football plot is shown in Figure 5.3 (stylized from the actual computer output for simplicity), which relates to the merger project whose QRA S-curve results are given in Figure 5.2.

Each of the points in the "football" indicates one possible individual cost-time output (an iteration) resulting from running the simulation model, with a value for how much the project might cost and when it might be completed. The boundary of the football is a best-fit calculation reflecting a given level of confidence (usually 90 percent). This means that 90 percent of the calculated cost-time pairs fall within the boundary. The center of gravity of the football indicates the expected cost and time outcomes. The results contained within the boundary match the information from standard S-curve outputs from simulations of cost variation and time variation, but these are combined in the football plot to show how the two variables are related. The earliest/latest project end dates in Figure 5.3 correspond to Figure 5.2a, lying between May and August of next year, and the range of cost results shown in Figure 5.3 between "minimum total cost" and "maximum total cost" equates to the

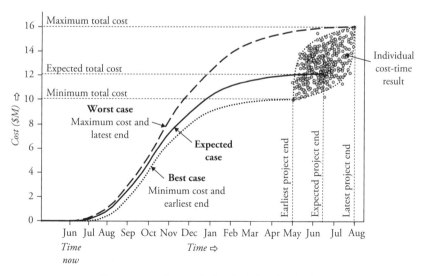

Figure 5.3: *Example football (eyeball) plot*

S-curve for cost variation between $10 million and $16 million in Figure 5.2b.

In addition to showing the range of possible cost-time endpoints for the merger project, Figure 5.3 also plots the paths that the merger project might follow toward reaching these outcomes. In fact, each of the many hundreds of individual cost-time results has a path leading to it from the "Time Now" start point, but for the purposes of simplicity and clarity, the football plot only shows three key paths:

- The best-case track that leads to the earliest end date and the minimum total cost
- The expected-case track that leads to the expected end date and the expected total cost
- The worst-case track that leads to the latest end date and the maximum total cost

The specific example football plot in Figure 5.3 relates to uncertainty in cost growth with time, but with a finite duration (the merger project), and the football contains the possible endpoints. It is, however, equally possible to produce similar outputs for other ongoing time-based variables, such as market share, share price, profit, and so on, where there is no fixed duration. This is achieved simply by removing the football endpoint from the plot, and showing only the range of possible tracks going forward from Time Now. There are of course an almost infinite number of potential future paths, so the plot presents two outer bounds with a central forecast.

Figure 5.4 provides an example, plotting uncertainty in cash flow going forward for several years. This example is based on a simple influence diagram, built from the various contributors to and consumers of cash flow. Possible variations in each contributing factor provide inputs to a probabilistic Monte Carlo simulation, with measurements taken of the resulting annual cash flow. This provides a range of possible cash flow results for each year, reflected in the spread seen in Figure 5.4. The upper and lower values for cash flow in each year represent the 95 percent and 5 percent confidence points respectively from the simulation, with a central mean value also plotted.

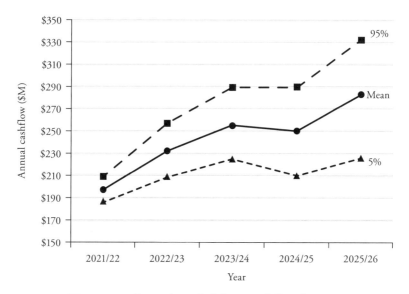

Figure 5.4: *Example probabilistic cash flow forecast*

These three values are effectively taken from an S-curve of values at the end of each simulated year.

Comparing Figures 5.3 and 5.4 for a Risk Hurricane with Figure 5.1 for a natural hurricane, the similarities are immediately evident. The risk analyst's football plots and probabilistic forecast plots bear a striking resemblance to the meteorologist's cone of uncertainty. All these figures show the increasing range of possible outcomes associated with moving into the future from the current position at Time Now, allowing decision-makers to estimate the degree of uncertainty that they might face at a given moment.

USING RISK INFORMATION TO MANAGE THE RISK HURRICANE

You might have found some of the preceding detailed discussion about risk modeling hard to follow, especially if you're not a risk expert. The typical senior leader knows the importance of balancing risk exposure with potential benefit when making key decisions, but they're not familiar with the internal workings of complex risk models. This means that you likely won't know how to produce a football plot or probabilistic forecast chart. But this need not stop you using these powerful report formats to support your risk-based decision-making. A competent risk practitioner will know how to build the underlying risk models that generate these outputs, and they will also be able to guide you in interpreting their meaning. Or as a minimum, your in-house risk colleagues can enlist the support of external risk experts to undertake the types of detailed analysis described previously.

Here again, the natural hurricane analogy comes to our aid. Joe Public will never understand how complex meteorological models produce a cone of uncertainty, nor does he need to do so. The friendly TV weather forecaster is on screen to make sense of it all, explaining the map in simple terms and providing actionable guidance on what you should do. Based on the current analysis, local authorities issue hurricane watch bulletins and hurricane warnings, instructing residents and businesses initially to prepare for disruption, and ultimately to take necessary avoidance or protective action.

In a business facing the potential of major disruption from a Risk Hurricane, risk specialists must perform the same vital roles, explaining the meaning of key analytical outputs, and interpreting them into warnings and recommendations for appropriate action.

So how do you use the football plot or a probabilistic forecast chart? The key aspect of these outputs is that they are predictive, providing reliable information about the likely future behavior of an impending Risk Hurricane. Knowing what you know now, and starting from where you currently are, these charts indicate how things might develop as time passes and where they could ultimately lead you. And if the prediction shows unacceptably high levels of risk exposure ahead, it also gives you time to act.

Taking Figure 5.3 as an example, you can identify from the diagram the point at which uncertainty starts to grow, indicated by the increased spread between the best-case and worst-case tracks. This appears to occur between October and November, about four months from Time Now. This tells you that you need to act in the coming three to four months to avoid or minimize the potential increase in risk exposure that is predicted to occur.

But what action should you take, and when? The purpose of risk analysis is to give early warning to decision-makers, enabling them to make necessary choices while there is still time to influence future events, and before the situation becomes so uncertain and stressful that suboptimal decisions are more likely. For natural hurricanes, warnings are issued well before hurricane conditions arrive, to enable people to make necessary preparations before they become too difficult. Senior leaders in an organization threatened by an impending Risk Hurricane need similar communication from their risk expert colleagues, based on the results of the latest analysis. The urgency of these communications is based on how soon we might expect the Risk Hurricane to arrive, and this is known as *risk proximity*. This is assessed using the following steps:

- Determine how soon the first adverse effects of a Risk Hurricane are expected to occur (impact window).
- Identify potential risk responses that would address these effects and when those responses must be implemented in order to be effective (action window).
- Estimate the relation in time between impact window and action window.
  - Where the action window is much earlier than the impact window, risk proximity is low, and there is plenty of time to implement the required risk responses.
  - Shorter gaps in time between action window and impact window indicate increasing risk proximity, and the urgency of responding increases correspondingly.
  - If the action window occurs in parallel with the impact window, or after the impact is expected to have begun, then the situation is critical since no proactive action can be taken.

Once we understand the proximity of the Risk Hurricane, we can issue appropriate advice to decision-makers on how and when to respond. For this, we might adopt the two-level communication model used for the natural hurricane:

- *Risk Hurricane watch.* This early warning report is used to tell senior leaders that current risk analysis shows the possibility of significant uncertainty ahead and that sufficient time is available to take necessary action to avoid impact and put protective measures in place.

- *Risk Hurricane warning.* By contrast, this type of report is an urgent call to action, stating that major business disruption is imminent and the organization needs to implement its predefined contingency plans in order to minimize the likely impact.

CASE STUDY: CLIMATE CHANGE MODELING

The discussion topic on everyone's lips in recent times seems to be climate change. Some people feel very strongly about this topic (on both sides of the debate), while for others it evokes real apathy. The current climate change conversation is a good example of the importance of prediction when considering the future possibility of extreme risk exposure that could cause major disruption. We all need to answer two key questions about climate change:

- Where is it going?
- How big will it be?

These are the same questions tackled by meteorologists analyzing the possible path of a natural hurricane, as well as by business analysts and leaders who recognize the development of an oncoming Risk Hurricane. We've seen in this chapter that both sets of experts use powerful modeling techniques to forecast alternative futures, providing valuable information on where disruption is likely and how severe it might be. Their two challenges are:

- To build truly representative models
- To communicate the results in a way that can be used by those affected

These same two challenges are faced by the experts who seek to provide a robust scientific basis for the climate debate. Forecasting changes in global climate is inherently complex, requiring sophisticated modeling, deep analysis, and careful interpretation. But the results of this analysis must be communicated in terms that can be widely understood by non-experts, giving them sound information that they can use to determine how significant the risk exposure might be and to decide what action is appropriate.

Climate modeling used to be subject to considerable skepticism over its reliability and validity. Perceptions have changed radically, however, with two pioneering climate modelers (Syukuro Manabe and Klaus Hasselmann) sharing the 2021 Nobel Prize for Physics with theoretical quantum physicist Giorgio Parisi.

The Intergovernmental Panel on Climate Change (IPCC) is the United Nations body for assessing the science related to climate change. The most recent version of the IPCC assessment report (IPCC, 2021) includes an annex on the models used to analyze climate change, assessing 66 Regional Climate Models (RCMs). IPCC has also issued guidance notes to the report's authors on how to handle and represent uncertainty consistently, recognizing that this is a key challenge (IPCC, 2005). These notes focus on how to reflect the level of confidence in the validity of findings, as well as how to express quantified measures of uncertainty.

Despite this careful approach, the public message about the likely effects of climate change is framed in one simple metric: the extent that the temperature of the earth's atmosphere is expected to rise above preindustrial levels, measured in degrees Celsius (°C). The Paris Agreement of 2015 set a target to limit global warming to 1.5°C, and the debate over whether the world is on track to meet this target or not is expressed in terms of dates and temperatures. The media, lobbyists, and environmental activists focus on just one output from climate change modeling: predicted changes in global temperature over time. Many other measurable indicators are available from the expert analysis, including changes in the polar ice cap, rising sea levels, greenhouse gas emissions, levels of carbon dioxide and methane, ocean temperature, and so on. But public consciousness is focused around "global warming" in degrees Celsius.

Many of the disagreements in the climate conversation arise from this oversimplification. Hundreds of talented people are working with multiple complex models, taking data from a wide range of global sources and combining the outputs into a consensus view that reflects the inherent uncertainty in the models and their interpretation. In-depth detailed analysis done properly by genuine experts produces robust and reliable results. But this huge amount of work is then distilled into a single number, which can be hard to translate into action. If global temperatures are predicted to rise by 2.4°C by 2050, instead of staying at or below 1.5°C, what should individuals, communities, businesses, and nations do about it? People need to be able to trust the experts to have done the hard work in the background, but they also need actionable information that they can use to inform their decisions and to shape their future behavior.

Future climate change shows all the characteristics of a Risk Hurricane, with the possibility of extreme risk exposure that would lead to disruption on a global scale. The use of climate models allows experts to forecast the likely range of such exposure and to predict resulting levels of disruption, meeting the first challenge of determining how big the Risk Hurricane could be. Whether they are also meeting the second challenge, to communicate uncertainty in a way that allows people to respond appropriately, remains an open question.

CLOSING CONSIDERATIONS

Predicting the future trajectory and possible size of an oncoming Risk Hurricane requires sophisticated analysis using powerful tools. The advanced risk analysis techniques described in this chapter reflect the complex nature of Risk Hurricanes, involving multiple sources of uncertainty that combine together to create extreme risk exposure that can cause major business disruption. However, you may not need an intimate understanding of how quantitative risk analysis models work in practice.

If you're a risk specialist responsible for advising senior business leaders in your organization, you should at least be aware of these QRA techniques and either be proficient in their use yourself or be able to commission other risk experts to undertake such analyses on your behalf. You must also be able to translate outputs from in-depth risk analysis and turn them into actionable recommendations for your decision-making colleagues.

And if you're a senior leader, you need to know what type of information can be provided by this type of risk analysis. You should understand how to interpret the basic analytical outputs and be able to ask intelligent questions of your risk colleagues, such as:

- How much risk exposure do we face?
- Which areas of the business are most at risk?
- What are main drivers of risk exposure?
- Which are the biggest risks, including the worst threats and the best opportunities?
- How long have we got to respond?
- What are my options?

Answering these key questions will ensure that you can make the best possible preparations before a Risk Hurricane arrives, minimizing the potential for business disruption and giving your organization the best chance of surviving extreme risk exposure.

Preparedness

Weather forecasters work hard to predict the possible path of an oncoming natural hurricane and to issue timely communications to the public and businesses that might be affected. But the fast-moving nature of hurricanes means that such warnings are only issued when the hurricane is already close at hand. The cone of uncertainty predicts the possible path of the storm center for three to five days ahead. A hurricane watch tells people that a hurricane is possible, with storm-force winds expected in the coming 48 hours, and a hurricane warning gives 36 hours' notice. The short-term nature of these communications doesn't give much time for people and businesses to prepare, and any serious preparation must be done in advance.

Fortunately, good guidance exists for individuals, families, and businesses, outlining the sorts of preparation that are needed if you're located in an area where hurricanes are known to occur. But what about Risk Hurricanes? What advice is available to help us prepare in advance for the possibility of extreme risk exposure that leads to major business disruption? And what can we learn from natural hurricane preparation to improve and strengthen Risk Hurricane readiness?

In this chapter we introduce a new approach to vulnerability assessment, indicating where business leaders need to focus their short-term actions when preparing to face a Risk Hurricane. We also present proven frameworks for developing organizational resilience to provide longer-term protection against the effects of extreme risk exposure, and we explore how to use the novel concept of anti-fragility in practice.

PREPARING FOR A NATURAL HURRICANE

Given the frequency of hurricanes in certain areas of the world, most affected countries have developed comprehensive advice and guidance on how to prepare, both for members of the public and for businesses. Typical advice for individuals includes actions to be taken in advance of any hurricane warning to identify and reduce vulnerabilities, as well as things to do in the period immediately preceding the expected arrival of a hurricane, ensuring that the required resources are in place to support survival during the hurricane event. This usually includes the following areas:

- Strengthen home
- Check insurance
- Protect records
- Create emergency communications plan
- Assemble disaster supplies
- Prepare for evacuation

The advice to businesses facing an incoming natural hurricane is more structured, with a three-step approach to define a hurricane preparedness framework. Although this appears to be simple, it can require a significant degree of thought and work to do properly. The three steps are as follows:

- **Identify vulnerabilities.** A business owner might seek specialist advice to help them with identifying vulnerabilities, or they may be able to draw on generic guidelines from industry or government bodies. A better approach might be for a business to develop a specific checklist of vulnerable elements that relates to their own organization and to maintain and update this in the light of experience.
- **Plan preparedness and mitigation actions.** This also needs to be very specific, listing protective actions that can be taken in

advance, as well as mitigating actions that will be implemented when a hurricane is underway. Depending on the size of the business, a leader may develop a simple action plan that lists who will do what, how, using which resources, and by when. Or it may be appropriate to produce a series of separate stand-alone documents, including a Business Continuity Plan, a communications plan, a disaster response plan, and so on.

- **Implement actions when required.** This vital step requires the organization to take timely actions to complete protective measures as soon as practically possible, and certainly before the next hurricane season. Necessary resources should also be gathered in advance to enable mitigating measures to be implemented effectively and fast in the event of a hurricane approaching.

These three steps of Identify/Plan/Implement should be considered across five important aspects of the organization:

- **People.** Consider impacts and implications for your people. This might include direct employees and their family members, as well as subcontractors and suppliers. Include both physical protection and emotional/psychological well-being at work, as well as considering their ability to travel to work or the possibility of functioning remotely.
- **Property (buildings).** Review your buildings to identify weak spots that might suffer damage. Pay particular attention to roofs, windows, and doors. Identify any key access points that might become blocked or unavailable due to hurricane damage.
- **Property (grounds).** Evaluate possible effects on your property, including trees, fences, landscaping, signage, phone masts, and so on.
- **Property (workspace).** Review contents of the working areas, including offices, document stores, shopfloor, goods inward, storage areas, and production lines. Think about the possible effect of high winds or floods on furniture and fittings, filing cabinets, shelving, tools, machinery, and so on.

- **Practical support systems.** Consider possible impacts on both utilities (electricity, gas, internet, water, sanitation, lights, heating, air-conditioning, fuel storage) and technological systems (computers, copiers, telephones, payroll, alarm systems, specialist equipment).

Having developed a hurricane readiness plan, the wise business leader will test it out before it is needed for real. This might involve a simple desk exercise, or computer-based simulations, or real-world practice drills. This allows fine-tuning of the plan before it is used in a real hurricane situation.

It's also important to review the plan on a regular basis, perhaps annually, to ensure that the information is current, correct, and complete. Contact details in the communications plan may have changed, with different individuals or new telephone numbers and email addresses. It is quite likely that vulnerabilities might change with time or that new or different protective or mitigating actions might be required. It's also possible that additional actions might be needed as a result of changes to identified vulnerabilities and planned responses.

Each of these steps has parallels for the business wishing to prepare in advance for the possible arrival of a Risk Hurricane.

PREPARING FOR A RISK HURRICANE

Unless your business is situated in a hurricane-prone location, you won't need to follow the guidance outlined in the previous section, as this is only relevant to individuals and organizations who find themselves in an area where natural hurricanes occur. Fortunately, this isn't most of us.

Unfortunately, things are very different when it comes to Risk Hurricanes. Every business is vulnerable to the possibility of extreme risk exposure that could lead to major disruption. For your business and mine, it's a case of *when* not *if*. This means that we all need to consider how to prepare ourselves and our organization in advance, to give ourselves the best possible chance of surviving the next Risk Hurricane and being able to recover after it has passed.

The basic steps to take when preparing for a Risk Hurricane match those required for a natural hurricane, namely:

- **Identify vulnerabilities.**
- **Plan preparedness and mitigation actions.**
- **Implement actions in a timely manner.**

Most of these elements are covered by business continuity planning (BCP), which is a well-established discipline. A full description of BCP is beyond the scope of this book, and detailed guidance is available elsewhere, notably from the *Business Continuity Institute* (Business Continuity Institute, 2013). However, it's useful to be more specific about particular elements of Risk Hurricane preparedness, as discussed below.

IDENTIFY VULNERABILITIES

Each business is unique, and the areas that are most at risk of major disruption from a Risk Hurricane will differ from one organization to another. It may therefore seem impossible or unwise to attempt to give general advice on how to define particular areas of vulnerability that will be relevant to your organization. However, regardless of the specifics of your business, it's helpful to use a structured framework when considering where you might be most exposed to high levels of risk. This will help to protect you against the effects of bias when considering where your organization might be most exposed to risk.

Beating Bias

It's important when preparing for the extreme risk exposure of a Risk Hurricane that you maintain as wide a focus as possible. This means thinking outside the box, taking account of the areas of vulnerability that come immediately to mind, of course, but also being creative and looking proactively and intentionally in the places that you usually overlook. Churchill wrote, "It is a joke in Britain to say that the War Office is always preparing for the last war" (Churchill, 1948); we do tend to focus our protection efforts on the areas where we were most recently affected. But Taleb pointed out, "If humans fight the last war, nature fights the next one" (Taleb, 2012). It is the unexpected areas of vulnerability that will cause you the greatest trouble, when the extreme risk exposure of a Risk Hurricane strikes you in an area that you didn't realize was weak and exposed.

All of us are subject to influences that tend to narrow our perspective (Hillson & Murray-Webster, 2007; Murray-Webster & Hillson, 2008), raising the danger that we miss a significant area of vulnerability. Many of these biases are subconscious, making them harder to spot and address, including the following:

- *Availability*: more memorable or more recent events are treated as more significant (even if they're not)
- *Representativeness*: similarity to stereotypes seems like a reliable indicator of significance
- *Anchoring and adjustment*: the initial estimate feels most likely, even if it has no objective basis in fact
- *Confirmation trap*: seeking and weighting evidence that substantiates a prior conviction, and ignoring contrary data
- *Groupthink*: the majority view (real or perceived) suppresses expression of alternatives
- *Hero worship*: inappropriate weight is given to the view of an influential person
- *Cultural conformity*: the perceived organizational ethos or cultural norms limit choices
- *Illusion of control*: risk appears to be reduced by (real or perceived) ability to influence events
- *Lure of choice*: the ability to exercise choice is perceived as reducing risk
- *Optimism bias*: irrational view that things will go better than experience or data suggest
- *Precautionary principle*: preference to take action "just in case"

In addition to these subconscious influences, we're sometimes misled by rational factors that we think are more relevant than they really are, including:

- *Familiarity*: previous experience should be a reliable indicator of how well we'll be able to manage similar risks
- *Manageability*: risks that we can influence feel less severe than those over which we have no control
- *Proximity*: risks that are closer in time seem more important than those that are further off
- *Personal propinquity*: risk exposure is proportional to the extent to which something matters to me or us

When you're trying to identify areas of vulnerability for your business, you need to be aware of these influences and try to reduce their effect wherever you can. Each source of bias tends to narrow your focus, but you need to have as wide a preparedness perspective as possible. Being aware of the possibility of bias will help you to overcome its influence, through the exercise of emotional literacy and intentional choices. Another effective and proven way to counter the subjectivity that results from bias is to use a structured framework to guide your considerations, making it less likely that you'll miss something important. Two possible structured approaches are recommended to help you beat the biases when seeking to identify areas of vulnerability: *stress testing* and *sustainability analysis*.

Stress Testing

One common approach for finding vulnerabilities is to stress test the strategic objectives and critical functions of the organization, taking each objective and function in turn, and exploring how susceptible it is to significant variation above or below the normal range of conditions. This approach begins with defining risk thresholds against each strategic objective or function that state the outer bounds of acceptable performance. Risk thresholds reflect your risk appetite, providing a measurable indication of "How much risk is too much risk" for each objective/function.

Once you've defined risk thresholds, there are two possible indications that an objective or critical function might be particularly vulnerable to the high levels of risk exposure associated with a Risk Hurricane:

- Pay attention to any areas where the gap between upper and lower risk thresholds is narrow. In these cases, there's not much room for performance variation before a threshold is breached.
- Consider how close current performance is to the upper or lower risk threshold. Where you're already running near the boundary, it might not take much to push you over the edge.

For each vulnerable strategic objective or critical function, identify drivers of performance, and assess how they might change if risk exposure were significantly higher or lower than it is currently. The aim is to understand where high levels of uncertainty could drive performance beyond the limits of your risk appetite for that objective/function. When you find a strategic objective or critical function that might be particularly vulnerable to the effect of uncertainty, you can focus your attention in these areas of the business.

This approach can be refined further by completing a similar assessment for lower-level objectives and functions, allowing a structured and hierarchical view of where vulnerability exists across the organization. If you've implemented enterprise risk management (ERM) in your business, this provides an ideal framework for multi-level stress testing, analyzing vulnerability across the various levels from strategic to tactical.

Sustainability Analysis

A more generic way of finding key vulnerabilities is based on the Five Capitals of Sustainability. These define five areas that contribute to the production of value by an organization and must be protected and managed sustainably. They were first expressed in 2007 by the *Forum for the Future* (n.d.), as follows:

1. *Natural Capital.* This represents the environmental and ecological resources that are needed to produce goods or deliver services. They include energy, water, fuels, raw materials, and other natural resources, as well as the ecosystems from which these are taken.

2. *Human Capital.* This is not just about individuals as productive working resources, but it also covers their energy, health and well-being, knowledge and skills, motivations, and emotions.
3. *Social Capital.* This describes the way that people interact in the various teams within organizations. It is also about how people relate through other networks, partnerships, and less formal groupings. In some industries, this can include relations with local communities or pressure groups.
4. *Manufactured Capital.* This covers material goods and infrastructure that are used by an organization to generate its products and services but are not part of the delivered output. It includes buildings, machines, tools, communications networks, IT systems, and so on.
5. *Financial Capital.* These are assets that exist in currency form, including cash, shares, bonds, and loans.

Each of these Five Capitals forms part of the value chain that an organization uses to generate its goods and services. The challenge for the leadership of each business is to make decisions that use these different types of capital in a way that is wise, efficient, effective, and sustainable. The Five Capitals of Sustainability can help you to identify and assess areas of organizational vulnerability because they describe elements that are required in order to create value, and any impact on one of the Five Capitals would affect the ability of your business to function well.

The process for exposing areas of vulnerability is different from that used for stress-testing strategic objectives, since it focuses instead on the resources required for the organization to function effectively and sustainably. The first step is to describe each of the Five Capitals in more detail, listing within each category the specifics that are needed by your organization. This can be done at different levels of detail, but usually you'll start by seeking to understand your vulnerabilities at a high strategic level, allowing you to drill down into further detail for those areas that are found to be most exposed.

Next, you need to assess each of the contributing factors within the Five Capitals in two dimensions. The first considers how critical

Table 6.1: Example definitions of criticality and availability

	Criticality		Lack of Availability
VLO (1)	**Non-essential**. The business can function well even if this resource is limited or absent.	VLO (1)	**Unrestricted**. This resource is freely available in the quantity and quality required.
LO (3)	**Important**. Lack of this resource would impose some limitations on performance.	LO (2)	**Generally available**. In normal times, there are no restrictions in supply of this resource.
MED (5)	**Required**. Significant difficulties would arise if this resource were limited.	MED (3)	**Constrained**. Some conditions exist that limit availability of this resource.
HI (7)	**Business-critical**. The business is unable to perform in the absence of this resource.	HI (4)	**Severely limited**. Special arrangements are required to obtain this resource.

the specific resource is to the successful and sustainable functioning of your organization. Second, think about how available each resource is currently (or more properly, where there might be problems with lack of availability). The most vulnerable resources are those that are highly critical to the organization but have limited availability. Each level of criticality and availability must be defined unambiguously to avoid subjective disagreements over how to assess a particular resource, as illustrated in Table 6.1. Assessments of each resource can then be reflected using a two-dimensional "vulnerability assessment matrix," which may incorporate a simple scoring scheme to calculate a "vulnerability index" for prioritization, such as the example shown in Figure 6.1. This example has four levels of criticality and four degrees of availability, but you may choose to use more or fewer levels.

PLAN PREPAREDNESS AND MITIGATION ACTIONS

When you understand which areas of your business are most vulnerable to the effects of a Risk Hurricane, it's time to decide how to respond. Actions generally fall under three headings:

- Short-term preemptive preparation and protection
- Short-term reactive and recovery responses
- Longer-term structural changes

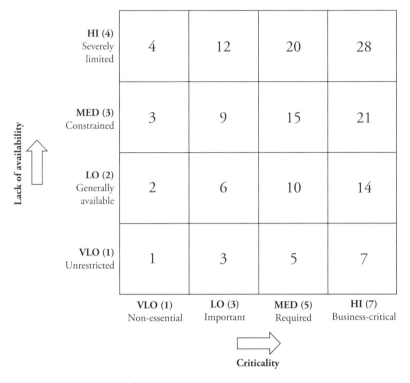

HI (4) Severely limited	4	12	20	28
MED (3) Constrained	3	9	15	21
LO (2) Generally available	2	6	10	14
VLO (1) Unrestricted	1	3	5	7

Lack of availability

| **VLO (1)** Non-essential | **LO (3)** Important | **MED (5)** Required | **HI (7)** Business-critical |

Criticality

Figure 6.1: *Example vulnerability assessment matrix*

Preemptive and reactive elements usually form part of a typical Business Continuity Plan, although some aspects of recovery may be addressed separately in a disaster recovery plan. The key for both preemptive and reactive planning is to consider what options you have in order to address specific individual vulnerabilities you've identified, then choose which options to implement, then plan when and how to take action.

Generic structural changes involve considering what changes you might make to the structure and nature of your organization in order to improve your chances of surviving a Risk Hurricane and thriving afterward. This approach is more generic than what is usually covered by business continuity planning.

Short-Term Preemptive Actions

Preemptive preparation and protection responses correspond to the actions taken by individuals and businesses threatened by a natural hurricane, strengthening your home or business premises, and protecting or moving items that are particularly exposed. It also involves checking insurance, ensuring that vital records are protected, and creating an emergency communications plan that identifies who to contact.

For each key vulnerability that you've identified for your business, consider what you can do in advance to protect against breaching a risk threshold on a strategic objective or a critical function and to protect against losing availability of a required resource.

Where vulnerability arises from a narrow risk threshold, consider whether your risk appetite in this area is appropriate. You and your senior management colleagues may intentionally decide to accept more variation in a strategic objective or to widen the acceptable bounds of performance for a critical function in order to allow more room for maneuver if/when risk exposure increases.

In cases where significant vulnerability exists for a key resource, consider building in redundancy, duplication, or contingency, changing processes to introduce additional slack or remove bottlenecks, or training additional staff to avoid single-point responsibilities. For resources where availability may become limited, additional supplies might be obtained and stockpiled, or new suppliers and providers could be sought.

Short-Term Reactive and Recovery Responses

These are comparable to steps taken by individuals or business owners to assemble disaster supplies and prepare to evacuate. The goal is to have required resources in place before they are needed and to define in advance what will need to be done in the event of a hurricane. This avoids the "What shall we do?" panic, allowing necessary predefined actions to be implemented calmly and effectively.

The equivalent for your business when preparing for a Risk Hurricane is to pre-position any recovery assets that will be needed and clarify actions to be taken. You need to provide sufficient detail that the people responsible for taking action will know precisely what to do. When you're in the midst of a Risk Hurricane, you don't want to be making important decisions on how to react. Apart from the inevitable delay that this would introduce, the unusual circumstances of extreme risk exposure and major business disruption make it very hard to take good decisions.

Longer-Term Structural Changes

In addition to specific preemptive and reactive actions that you identify to address individual vulnerabilities, you need to prepare your organization to face types of risk exposure that you've never seen before. Planned short-term responses aim to protect and mitigate against specific foreseen areas of vulnerability that you've identified in your business. In the longer term however, you need to be able to survive the unforeseeable, including emergent risks (International Risk Governance Council, 2010) and Black Swans (Taleb, 2007). Fortunately, there are two generic structural types of response that address risks that you haven't yet seen coming: *resilience* and *antifragility*. Both of these approaches target the characteristics of your organization as a whole, aiming to identify areas that can be changed in advance of a Risk Hurricane in order to improve your chances of surviving and thriving afterward, no matter what the future throws at you.

Resilience

The subject of resilience is well established, with many resources available that provide guidance and advice. However, despite this widespread interest, there is still no accepted definition of the term. The United Nations Office for Disaster Risk Reduction (UNDRR) defines resilience as "the ability of a system, community or society exposed to hazards to resist, absorb, accommodate, adapt to, transform and recover from the effects of a hazard in a timely and efficient manner, including through the preservation and restoration of its essential basic structures and functions through risk management" (UNDRR, n.d.). This definition has been applied in a variety of settings, from disaster risk reduction to society as a whole (House of Lords, 2021). When thinking about Risk Hurricanes, however, we're interested in how resilience applies to *organizations*.

The international standard ISO 22316:2017 *Security and resilience—Organizational resilience—Principles and attributes* defines organizational resilience as the "ability of an organization to absorb and adapt in a changing environment" (International Organization for Standardization, 2017), and the American National Standard ASIS SPC.1-2009 *Organizational Resilience* says it is "the adaptive capacity of an organization in a complex and changing environment," noting that "Resilience is the ability of an organization to resist being affected by an event or the ability to return to an acceptable level of performance in an acceptable period of time" (ASIS International, 2009).

However, practitioners frequently adopt a narrower view. They either focus merely on being able to cope with stress and adversity, or they consider only negative aspects such as the ability to absorb change without fracturing or breaking. It is common to think of resilience as the ability to recover back to the original condition after a force has caused some deformation or distortion. Alternative terms include "elasticity," "suppleness," "flexibility," or "bouncebackability." While these meanings might be useful in physics, ecology, or psychology, a different sense is developing in the field of organizational management.

For example, the Institute of Risk Management (IRM) report *Organisational Resilience: A Risk Manager's Guide* (2021) defines organizational resilience with two elements (Operational Resilience and Strategic Resilience), each with three sub-elements (see Figure 6.2). The activities commonly associated with resilience are grouped under Operational Resilience, focusing on processes that deliver protection

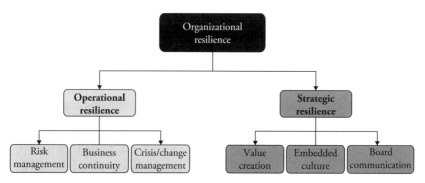

Figure 6.2: *IRM Organisational Resilience Framework*
(Adapted from Institute of Risk Management, 2021. Used with permission.)

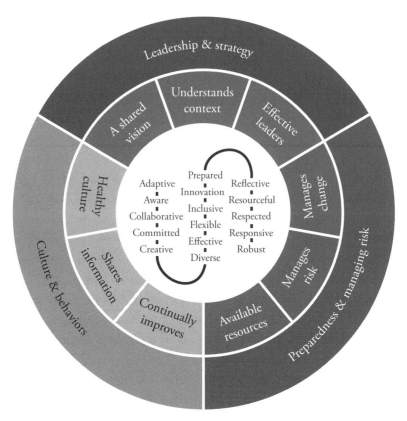

Figure 6.3: *ICOR Organizational Resilience Model*

and recovery. But the heading of Strategic Resilience covers other non-process aspects that are equally important.

Similarly, The International Consortium for Organizational Resilience (ICOR, https://www.build-resilience.org/) has developed useful guidelines, including a number of resilience frameworks, certifications, and credentials. The ICOR approach to organizational resilience has three dimensions (Leadership & Strategy, Culture & Behaviors, and Preparedness & Managing Risk), each of which is subdivided into three strategies, supported by a set of 16 behaviors (see Figure 6.3). As with the IRM framework, process-based elements are included, but more emphasis is placed by the ICOR model on leadership and culture.

The IRM and ICOR models of organizational resilience both include other elements outside the traditional disciplines of risk management, business continuity, and disaster recovery. They both mention "softer" aspects, including culture, behavior, communication, leadership, and strategy. This reflects the distinction made above between actions to address specific vulnerabilities through preemptive protection and reactive recovery, and the more generic approaches that involve the whole organization. These two models suggest that it's not enough to focus on *what we can do* through strong risk management and business continuity management. We also need to pay attention to *who we are*, expressed in our culture and behaviors.

The challenge of building a resilient culture with flexible supporting behaviors is not trivial. It is much easier to concentrate instead on process-based solutions. But these will only help us to address the immediate issues arising from a Risk Hurricane, using protection and recovery strategies. Wise leaders will spend time and effort in developing longer-term solutions that will make their organizations more resilient. The characteristics of such a resilient culture have been defined by the New Zealand–based Resilient Organisations research consortium (see https://www.resorgs.org.nz/), with a set of 13 indicators that can be measured to determine your degree of organizational resilience. These "resilience indicators" are shown in Figure 6.4, arranged under three headline attributes: Leadership & Culture, Networks & Relationships, and Change Ready.

The prominence of softer aspects of culture and behaviors in these three models makes it clear that actions aimed at increasing resilience must be planned and implemented as part of the strategic development of your organization. As such, they clearly address issues that are much wider than your preparedness for a Risk Hurricane.

Antifragility

The term "antifragility" was coined by Nassim Nicholas Taleb in his book *Antifragile: Things That Gain from Disorder* (Taleb, 2012). While this concept has attracted considerable interest, it's still not entirely clear how it can be used practically within organizations. We include it here to stimulate thinking outside the usual box of

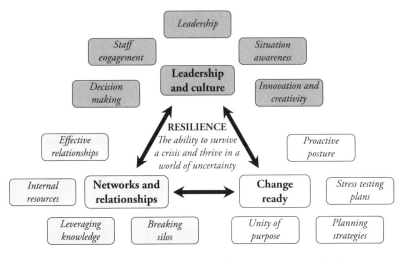

Figure 6.4: _Characteristics of a resilient organizational culture_
(From Seville, 2016. Used with permission.)

risk management, business continuity, and resilience. The idea of antifragility suggests a different way of thinking about how we might respond to the challenge of major business disruption in ways that bring positive improvement.

The concept arises by imagining a spectrum of possible ways to handle the challenge of external forces, as illustrated in Figure 6.5. This shows the end-points that result from each of three approaches to handling disruption, indicating where we might end up if/when the strategy fails.

The first set of responses comes under the heading of Strength. By making our organization strong, we can resist the pressures that might otherwise force us to change in ways that aren't consistent with our preferred way of working. The stronger we are, the more we can handle pressure. The problem comes when we run out of strength, and when external forces break through our defenses. The result is failure, as we collapse in the face of the challenge, which ultimately results in loss of value. Strength as a strategy for dealing with disruptive force is an all-or-nothing binary approach. We're either strong enough to resist the challenge, or we're not. If we con-

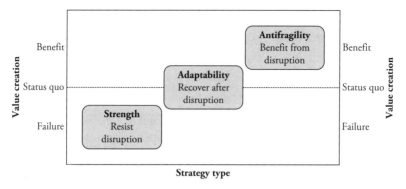

Figure 6.5: *End-points resulting from Strength, Adaptability and Antifragility responses to disruption*

sider the types of action that we can take to protect ourselves in advance from disruption or to define effective recovery plans to be implemented afterward, these are all Strength responses designed to help us ward off the effects of a Risk Hurricane. Things are good while these responses work as planned, but if they fail, then we suffer the full negative effects of disruption.

A second type of response is Adaptability. This is classic resilience territory. The Japanese proverb "The bamboo that bends is stronger than the oak that resists" illustrates the difference between Adaptability and Strength strategies. Adaptability starts by accepting the deformation that results from the external forces of change, trusting that we'll be able to recover when the situation returns to normal. The term "bouncebackability" captures this well. The weakness is that Adaptability responses aim to return us to normal, regaining our original shape and purpose after the forces of disruption cease. But sometimes the situation will also have changed in ways that make our original shape and purpose less relevant than it was previously. In these cases, we need to find new ways of working that maintain our core purpose and vision, or maybe we'll have to change our purpose.

Antifragility is positioned as a progression from the responses of Strength and Adaptability. Instead of resisting the forces of change (Strength) or accepting them and then seeking to recover

(Adaptability), Antifragility welcomes disruption and disorder as an opportunity to create positive improvement and change. This is partly reflected in the proverb "What doesn't kill you makes you stronger" (which isn't strictly true, as disruption can leave you weakened or wounded), but antifragility goes further. It reflects situations that *require* disorder or disruption in order to reach their full potential, and that benefit from stress. The adaptive immune system is a good example, since effective antibodies can only be produced in the presence of the antigen threat. Child development is antifragile, since learning comes from experience, including both bad and good. Broken bones are stronger after healing than they were before. And some non-Newtonian fluids turn to solid when shaken or stressed, including custard that becomes strong enough to walk on when it experiences the pressure of a person's weight.

Each of these four examples has parallels in organizations seeking antifragile ways to respond to the major business disruption of a Risk Hurricane:

- *Adaptive immune system.* Antigens activate an antibody response that deals with the immediate challenge and also provides ongoing protection against this and similar threats. Empowered individuals and teams can act like antibodies, if they have clear scope, defined boundaries of action and authority, and preallocated resources. They need to be alert and agile, poised for action and ready to go when the challenge arises. And having responded once, they'll be more motivated and capable to respond again if a similar situation arises in future.

- *Child development.* When innovation and experimentation are combined with a robust approach to capturing lessons, failure becomes valuable. This requires a safe space within which to operatc, encouraging confidence and freedom to try new things. The debrief process is also crucial to ensure that benefits are gained from experiences that others might find negative, demotivating, or damaging.

- *Broken bones.* The body recognizes that damage has occurred and initiates a staged repair process, from an initial blood clot at the fracture site to laying down soft tissue across the fracture, then replacing tissue over time with new solid bone. Where an organization experiences a fracture, time and resources should be provided to build across the gap, adopting a phased approach that gradually increases strength, ultimately going beyond what was originally present.

- *Non-Newtonian fluids.* These change state when pressure is applied, increasing viscosity in a way that allows them to support weight. This occurs when particles in suspension are forced together into a semisolid structure. In organizations experiencing pressure, people can be forced to interact in new ways that increase creativity and encourage synergy, improving efficiency and allowing the additional pressure to be absorbed productively.

While the concept of antifragility has been around for over a decade, its application is still in its infancy. However, for businesses prepared to explore and experiment, it offers new options for building an organization that is structured to survive and thrive in the face of a Risk Hurricane. And although the benefits of being antifragile are only seen when stress and pressure are applied, the preparatory work to build antifragility into your organization must be completed in advance.

Documenting Plans

At this point you'll have decided on *proactive preparatory actions* that offer protection in advance for your key vulnerabilities, as well as defining *reactive recovery actions* to be implemented in the event that a Risk Hurricane occurs, and considering *generic structural changes* to the organization to improve your chances of surviving and thriving. But deciding is not doing. You need to document your decisions and plans in sufficient detail to enable them to be implemented.

Plans for preemptive preparation and reactive responses can be documented in a Business Continuity Plan so that you can communicate them to affected stakeholders, particularly those individuals who will be required to implement actions. Various Business Continuity Plan templates are available, all sharing similar characteristics, and the format is less important than the act of recording decisions and communicating agreed-upon actions. Whichever format is adopted, the Business Continuity Plan must answer the six key questions made famous by Rudyard Kipling in the opening lines of his poem *The Elephant's Child* (Kipling, 1902):

> *I keep six honest serving-men*
> *(They taught me all I knew);*
> *Their names are What and Why and When*
> *And How and Where and Who.*

Any meaningful plan of action should address each of these elements:

- *What* will be done. Provide a SMART description of the action (specific, measurable, achievable, relevant, timely).
- *Why* it should be done. Clearly specify the purpose of the action.
- *When* it will be done. For preemptive actions, give a deadline for completion, together with interim milestone dates where appropriate. It's helpful to divide reactive actions into those that require implementing immediately, short-term actions to be undertaken in the first few days, and other tasks to be completed later.
- *How* it will be done. Outline required methods, processes, tools, techniques, resources, and so on.
- *Where* it will be done. This might be a physical location, or more likely it describes the parts of the organization involved in performing the action.
- *Who* will do it. Each action needs a single responsible owner who is accountable for its completion, and other contributors may also be specified (possibly using a RACI chart to define who is Responsible, Accountable, Contributing/Consulted, and Informed).

The Business Continuity Plan is not merely a record of the planning stage; instead it is an action plan that will be used to help you and your colleagues know what must be done now, before there's any hint that a Risk Hurricane may be on its way. It will also guide your responses when you receive warning that a Risk Hurricane is approaching, and it will tell you what must be done as the crisis of major business disruption unfolds around you.

Outside the Business Continuity Plan, you also need to create an action plan for implementing decisions that increase organizational resilience, as well as changes that could introduce elements of anti-fragility. Because these approaches are generic, you may need to launch a strategic initiative or business improvement program to facilitate the required changes to the organization. These could involve process modifications, changes to staffing numbers or balance of skills, behavioral adjustments, or developments in cultural values and beliefs.

Having documented your planned actions, it's important that you test your plans to check whether there might be any glitches, aspects where you've missed an important step or duplicated something unintentionally. This can usually be done in a desk-based review or a computer-based simulation, but you might also want to execute a dummy run of elements of your plan to see how they work out in practice. Where you discover weaknesses in the plan, work to fix them then retest to ensure that the problem is resolved.

It's also important that completed plans shouldn't sit untouched or unread on the shelf for years. You should undertake regular reviews of your plans to be sure that they remain relevant and achievable. Check whether the actions you previously defined will still be effective. Are your prepositioned resources still available? Has staff turnover made some elements of your plan unworkable, and do you need to nominate and/or train replacements? Perhaps new approaches have been developed within your organization or elsewhere in the industry that offer improved effectiveness over what you'd initially planned.

IMPLEMENT ACTIONS

As with all aspects of a risk-based approach to business, analysis must lead to action to achieve full benefit. This is obviously true when preparing for the possible arrival of a Risk Hurricane.

Each of the actions documented in the Business Continuity Plan must be implemented in a timely manner. In some cases, this will mean taking action well in advance of any possible disruption, especially where protective or reactive measures may take time to put in place or to become embedded and effective. In other cases, it might be appropriate to wait until a Risk Hurricane is imminent before acting to ensure that maximum protection is achieved.

The same is true for actions aimed at producing resilience or antifragility. These may have been documented in a strategic review report or business improvement plan, or they may be part of an ongoing strategic initiative or cultural development program. Helpful implementation guidance is available from a variety of sources, including the report *Resilience Reimagined: A Practical Guide for Organisations* commissioned by the UK National Preparedness Commission (Deloitte, 2021), which proposes a range of practices for developing resilience. These include:

- Consider and discuss the possibility of future failure as a learning opportunity
- Identify relationships and connectivity between apparently unrelated areas of the business
- Understand how value is created and delivered by the business
- Clearly define risk thresholds for objectives across all levels of the organization
- Regularly use stress testing to validate thresholds and modify them where required
- Adopt adaptive leadership styles that respond to current and changing circumstances

CASE STUDY:
PREPARING FOR ZERO-CARBON FUTURE

One of the most important things you can do for your business is to invest time, energy, and resources in preparing for a Risk Hurricane. We've seen in this chapter that three steps are required:

- Identify vulnerabilities.
- Plan preparedness and mitigation actions.
- Implement actions.

Thinking early about the possibility of major disruption allows you to be proactive in putting in place protective measures that maximize your chances of surviving extreme risk exposure and thriving once it has passed.

This is well illustrated by the approach adopted by major energy companies to the challenge of a zero-carbon future. Instead of burying their heads collectively in the (oil-bearing) sand, they've been considering their options and laying their plans for some time. The pace of preparation has increased recently as the zero-carbon Risk Hurricane approaches, and energy companies have started to publicize their plans more widely.

As one of the world's so-called "supermajor" oil and gas companies, the vulnerability of BP plc in a zero-carbon world is clear. As fossil fuels are phased out, the organization's raison d'être is under threat. BP's response is encapsulated in its current slogan "From IOC to IEC," expressing the strategic redirection to move from an international oil company to an integrated energy company. This will involve focusing on low-carbon energy projects, investing in offshore wind and solar energy, bioenergy, and hydrogen and aiming to reduce greenhouse gas emissions in operations. Hydrocarbons will remain part of the BP portfolio during the transition period, although there will be no new exploration, and BP aims to reduce the carbon intensity of its products, as well as greening its processes. The company is aiming for net zero across all operations by 2050, including upstream oil and gas production, and it is investing in carbon capture, utilization, and storage (CCUS) to reduce emissions.

Each of these steps plays a part in preparing BP to face the uncertainty and disruption that a zero-carbon future will inevitably bring to an energy company, as well as putting measures in place to mitigate any negative impact. The various elements of the strategy include immediate and short-term changes that are being implemented right away, as well as longer-term pivots in the positioning and identity of BP as a corporation. Only time will tell whether its approach exhibits the characteristics of antifragility or whether it was merely adaptive (see Figure 6.5).

Perhaps the biggest challenge for BP lies in changing public perception. For most people, BP is still intimately associated with fossil fuels (the clue is in the name: the "P" in BP originally stood for "petroleum"). Spectacular disasters like Texas City (2005) and Deepwater Horizon/Macondo (2010) still loom large in public memory, creating a reputation deficit that requires attention. As the company seeks to transform itself in order to survive the coming zero-carbon Risk Hurricane, it needs to reposition the way it is viewed. Consequently, in addition to laying out the new strategy and detailed plans for its achievement, BP is undertaking a major communication exercise to raise awareness of the company's efforts. Implementation of the new approach has been underway since early 2020, and each milestone is highlighted in press releases, presentations, interviews, webcasts, and website updates.

CLOSING CONSIDERATIONS

Louis Pasteur said, "Chance favors the prepared mind," echoing Roman philosopher Lucius Annaeus Seneca, who said, "Luck is what happens when preparation meets opportunity." If you want your business to have optimal chances of surviving a Risk Hurricane with minimal damage, then you need to make the best possible preparations.

As you think about how to get ready, your planning should address two distinct time frames. The first aspect to consider is the long-term actions that are needed to maximize the resilience of your organization and perhaps also to build in some antifragile characteristics. You might imagine that you can leave long-term changes until later and that immediate and short-term actions should take higher priority. However, many of the most important changes may take some time to build into the way your organization operates, especially where they involve corporate culture, so the time to act is always now! Consider the following:

1. Review your current organizational culture against the 16 behaviors and 13 indicators in Figures 6.3 and 6.4. Determine which of these need to be strengthened in your organization in order for your culture to be truly resilient to the major business disruption that comes with a Risk Hurricane.

2. Design and launch a culture change program within the business, specifically focused on developing those behaviors and characteristics in which your corporate culture is less resilient. Nominate a change champion from your senior leadership team to spearhead the campaign, and ensure that you provide the necessary resources. Communicate frequently, celebrate success, and maintain momentum. Successful culture change can take two to three years to become embedded, so prepare for the long haul.

3. Review your business processes to identify elements that are fragile and might break easily when stressed. Explore ways of reinforcing these elements to improve their strength.

4. Look for creative approaches that might introduce antifragility into your culture, behavior, and processes, where stress can make you stronger. Consider options for "bouncing forward" rather than merely bouncing back to what you had before.

Having given significant attention to long-term strategic actions that improve your ability to survive a Risk Hurricane, you must also ensure that you are fully prepared tactically. This involves the following steps:

1. Identify areas of vulnerability in your business by stress testing your strategic objectives and critical functions to determine where current risk thresholds might be breached under duress. Also consider the possible impacts of extreme risk exposure against the Five Capitals, assessing and prioritizing each identified vulnerability.

2. Decide where it's possible to protect high-priority vulnerabilities by taking preemptive action in advance, and where you might need to be more reactive if and when necessary.

3. Design preemptive actions that you'll take when a Risk Hurricane appears on the horizon in order to protect vulnerable risk thresholds and to ensure continued availability of vulnerable resources. Develop reactive responses to be implemented in the event of a Risk Hurricane actually occurring, identifying in advance the actions you'll need to take and the resources that you'll need to have in place.

4. Document your decisions in a Business Continuity Plan, then use that to produce a detailed action plan for protective and reactive measures that includes information on when required actions must be implemented.

Completing these actions will ensure that you're as ready to face a Risk Hurricane as you can be. Your business will have developed maximum organizational resilience to resist and survive the effects of a Risk Hurricane, and it will also include antifragile elements that enable you to thrive as you move forward. All necessary protective measures will be in place to minimize damage to vulnerable areas, and your people will know what to do if the business actually encounters extreme risk exposure and major disruption.

All of this should make it easier for you to sleep at night, confident that you've done all you can to prepare for any Risk Hurricane that might threaten your business. But what if a Risk Hurricane actually occurs? What should you do afterward? It would be wise to plan in advance for the post-event recovery period so that you can do what must be done without delay.

SEVEN

Post-Event Responses

In the previous chapter, we thought about how you can prepare for the arrival of a Risk Hurricane in order to give your organization the best possible chance of survival. But if and when you experience a Risk Hurricane, what happens next?

This chapter considers what to do after the Risk Hurricane has passed. We provide a structured framework for damage assessment, and we explain the difference between immediate repairs and longer-term rebuilding. We also emphasize the importance of identifying and learning lessons from previous Risk Hurricanes to help us respond more effectively in future, and the key role of risk leadership in moving forward.

As with other chapters, we'll start by considering what you need to do if you're unfortunate enough to have been affected by a natural hurricane, then we'll turn our attention to the Risk Hurricane equivalents.

RECOVERING FROM A NATURAL HURRICANE

Individuals, communities, and businesses that have experienced a natural hurricane know that the hard work starts immediately after the storm has passed, with three phases of activity:

- Damage assessment
- Short-term repairs
- Longer-term rebuilding

Of course, these three steps apply to physical assets such as buildings, gardens, infrastructure, and so on. But it's equally (and arguably more) important to consider how people might have been affected by their experience of a hurricane.

Physical Assets

In the first phase of the post-hurricane response period, families and business owners return to the hurricane zone to see what has happened to their property. The level of impact will vary, from areas that are virtually unscathed to those that have escaped with only minor damage to buildings that have been completely destroyed. It's important for property owners to understand the full extent of the damage caused by the hurricane so that they can properly determine their next actions. These are divided into repairs that can be undertaken immediately or in the relative short term, allowing normal life to resume relatively quickly, and actions that will take considerably longer to complete.

The fortunate ones may be able to move back into their properties without delay and pick up where they left off, apart perhaps from a few days spent cleaning up the yard or repairing a few broken windows. Others may need to undertake more substantial work to fix broken and leaking roofs, repair damaged walls, clear blocked drains, or ensure that roads and paths are free from debris.

The less fortunate may also have experienced significant damage to the main external structure and/or interior of their buildings, perhaps from flooding, fires, blown-out windows, fallen trees, and so on. Perhaps essential services may have to be reconnected to restore power and water supplies or to ensure adequate telephone or internet facilities and functions. For those more severely affected, the property may have to be rebuilt either in part or completely, or in the worst case the damage may be irrecoverable and buildings may have to be abandoned. This may be equally true of domestic dwellings and community or commercial properties.

In addition, the local government will need to assess the damage to infrastructure, including roads and essential services.

The passage of a natural hurricane may not be all bad news, however. For some individuals or businesses, the dark clouds of a hurricane may have a silver lining. It can create unforeseen opportunities to improve the physical environment and infrastructure. As the storm passes over an area, it clears the ground, destroying any weak structures in its path. Where property must be repaired or rebuilt, we don't necessarily need to go back to what we had before. We can build stronger and more resilient structures or redesign our gardens and open spaces to be more attractive or useful. This requires an element of leadership and vision to see how things might be different after the storm, as well as the availability of resources and labor to enable the necessary work to be completed.

People

It's very easy for our attention to be focused on physical buildings and infrastructure when we're considering how to respond after a natural hurricane has occurred, and we frequently forget the human dimension. People will have been traumatized by their experiences, from the fear of impending catastrophe, through the event itself, and on into the uncertainty associated with the recovery phase. Some may have been injured physically, but more will be affected emotionally and psychologically. This includes those who chose to stay in place as well as those who felt the need to evacuate and leave property and possessions behind.

The sense of violation and insecurity that people feel after a natural disaster can have wide-ranging effects for a considerable time to come, influencing personal mood, close relationships, and the ability to function as an effective member of society and the community, as well as their performance in the workplace. Each of the three phases mentioned previously is also relevant to these human impacts, as we need to undertake a psychological "damage assessment" to understand where we and others might be suffering from adverse effects, before identifying the need for short-term "repairs" to provide necessary support, as well as possible longer-term "rebuilding" through professional treatment where required. We may need to pay particular attention to the most vulnerable, including infants and children, the elderly, and those with disabilities and special needs, bearing in mind that not all vulnerabilities are immediately evident to the casual observer.

RECOVERING FROM A RISK HURRICANE

Taking our lead from the natural hurricane, if your organization has experienced a Risk Hurricane, you should follow the same three-phase approach, starting with damage assessment, followed by short-term repairs and longer-term rebuilding. But you also need to remember to consider the effect of a Risk Hurricane on your people, focusing not only on more tangible assets.

DAMAGE ASSESSMENT

While it's self-evident that the first thing to do after experiencing major business disruption is to survey the impact, you may not always know where to start. A structured approach to damage assessment can make sure that you consider all the possible affected areas and don't overlook anything important. One way to achieve this is to use the vulnerability assessment that you undertook as part of your preparedness program and to check whether areas that you thought might be vulnerable have indeed been impacted. In Chapter 6, we introduced the Five Capitals as a framework for identifying key vulnerabilities, considering the following areas that contribute to the production of value:

1. Natural Capital, covering environmental and ecological resources
2. Human Capital, including all aspects of individuals in the organization
3. Social Capital, describing various interactions between people
4. Manufactured Capital, addressing material goods and infrastructure used in production
5. Financial Capital, which includes all currency-based assets

For each of the capitals, review those areas that you had previously identified as vulnerable and see whether the damage matched your prediction. In some cases, things might be better than you expected, with less impact from the disruption than you had feared. In other areas it might be worse. There may also be aspects of the business where the Risk Hurricane took a toll that you had not foreseen.

As with natural hurricanes, it's common for organizations to look first at the effects of disruption on things that are easy to measure or monitor, such as market share, supply chain, stock inventory, reputation, share price, capitalization, forward order book, and so on, and to forget about the effect on people (including yourself). By basing your damage assessment on the Five Capitals, you'll be sure to include individuals, teams, and the wider community, under the headings of Human Capital and Social Capital. It's important to exercise sensitivity and care in these areas, recognizing that individuals and groups may have been traumatized to a greater or lesser extent, and they may therefore react in unexpected and unpredictable ways. Larger organizations may wish to employ specialist consultants to explore the human impact of being exposed to extreme risk, gathering information in a confidential and compassionate way, with a nonconfrontational attitude that avoids blame or criticism. Such specialists may also be better able to recommend appropriate support for staff and other people who have been adversely affected by their experience of a Risk Hurricane.

SHORT-TERM REPAIRS

We saw in Chapter 6 that your preparations for a possible Risk Hurricane should include short-term preemptive actions aimed at protection of key vulnerabilities, as well as reactive responses designed to be carried out in the event of major disruption. You should already have implemented the preemptive measures in advance as part of your preparedness plan, but now that a Risk Hurricane has actually occurred, it's time to execute those reactive responses. In addition to the aspects that you'd identified in advance, your damage assessment will have identified other areas requiring immediate attention. You may address the implementation of these responses as part of a formal crisis management plan, or you may adopt a more ad hoc approach. Either way, it's time to take action.

For process-related areas such as supply chain, inventory, contractor availability, or performance, "repair" actions may be relatively straightforward. Financial impacts can be addressed through negotiations with banks, lenders, shareholders, or creditors, aiming to reschedule loan repayments or invoicing, raise additional capital, reduce costs, or improve cash generation.

Where you identify people issues in your post-Risk Hurricane damage assessment, these need careful and sensitive attention. Some of your colleagues may have experienced significant trauma during the period of disruption, leading to loss of confidence in their ability to perform. You may want to consider offering professional counseling to staff who demonstrate evidence of adverse impact on their mental health and well-being. Some staff may need to take additional sick leave for medical attention. Part-time or job-sharing working arrangements might be valuable for others as part of their recovery. It's important to maintain a caring culture toward those who are affected in this way, with no sense of blame or criticism. And as a leader in the organization, always remember that you're not immune from the effects of a Risk Hurricane, and you need to take care of yourself so that you can in turn take care of your colleagues.

The best way to ensure that post-event responses receive the required level of attention is to launch a fully resourced recovery project, with a designated senior and experienced project manager who is empowered to take the necessary action. The project plan should include both predefined reactive responses and newly identified actions, ensuring that these are coordinated in the most efficient and effective way to support rapid recovery of key functions, as well as supporting colleagues who have experienced adverse impacts.

LONGER-TERM REBUILDING

Following recent global economic shocks, many major organizations and some western governments have adopted the motto "Build back better," which at first sight would appear to be an appropriate goal for post-Risk Hurricane recovery. However, this slogan begs a question: What is meant by "better"?

If the goal is to build back the same as previously but just operating more efficiently (perhaps characterized as "faster, smarter, cheaper"), then one might question whether this is the best possible outcome following the cost of the global shock. An alternative suggestion might be that "better" should not merely mean to build back to the same objectives with more efficiency but to work toward different objectives that in themselves are better than the previous ones. If resilience can be described as "bouncebackability," the goal here might be instead to *bounce forward*.

This might prove to be useful advice for how to respond following any Risk Hurricane. The idea is to take the opportunity not just to restore what was lost as a result of extreme risk exposure and major business disruption but instead to build something different that is inherently better. This might mean serving the same customer base more completely, or it might mean developing new products for a different customer base, or indeed moving into a completely different business area. Any organization that decides to adopt "build back better" as a goal after a Risk Hurricane will have to consider how they define "better." This is most likely to be the result of a strategic review of vision, mission, and objectives, performed in the light of the new situation post-Risk Hurricane.

LEARNING LESSONS FOR THE FUTURE

Having experienced a Risk Hurricane and implemented your recovery plan, you might think you can relax and celebrate. But the post-event response phase is not yet complete. One of the most important tasks remains: to identify lessons that can be learned to ensure that your experience of future Risk Hurricanes is less painful.

Many organizations recognize the importance of learning lessons from the past in order to benefit the future. This is often supported by a process that involves undertaking reviews at key points in the business cycle to identify two types of areas for improvement:

- Aspects of performance that had gone well, which can be built upon in the future, and which might be incorporated into standard operating procedures

- Areas where performance had been below expectation or ineffective, and where remedial action is required to prevent recurrence

We usually refer to the output from this process as "lessons learned." But just because you identify something doesn't mean that future practice will take it into account. Lessons are only truly learned when they have been implemented in a future similar situation. As a result, we should really call these outputs "lessons-to-be-learned" (L2BL). This emphasizes the fact that something must change in our future behavior and practice as a result of identifying a lesson.

When you identify L2BL, you need to record each lesson in a form that can be used the next time a similar situation is encountered.

- Be specific in recording the trigger event or conditions that occurred previously and that led to the lesson being identified. This could be useful in spotting when a similar situation is arising and when this lesson might be relevant.
- Document the lesson-to-be-learned using clear and unambiguous language, including detailed actions to be taken.
- It's useful to record who identified this lesson and when, as a source of additional information and future reference if a similar situation arises.
- Nominate a person to take whatever actions are needed to ensure that the lesson-to-be-learned is actually learned (the "lesson owner").
- If possible, try to identify particular occasions when this lesson would be relevant, so that the lesson owner can be alert to the possibility of implementing the lesson in practice.

This information can be recorded in an L2BL Register, and Figure 7.1 provides a suggested format.

It's clearly important that business leaders should take every opportunity to review and improve performance, with a proactive process that aims to capture useful lessons. However, in practice many organizations don't have such a process, or where one exists it is not followed. In other cases, when a process is followed, it's seen as a

Lessons-to-Be-Learned Register

ID	Triggering Activity or Event	Lesson to Be Learned	Date Identified	Identified by	Lesson Owner	Next Implementation Opportunity	Expected Date to Implement

Figure 7.1: *Example Lessons-to-Be-Learned (L2BL) Register format*

box-ticking exercise of little value, or it's used merely to allocate blame or divert attention from existing weaknesses. If any of these describe your organization's position, you're wasting a valuable opportunity to learn from your Risk Hurricane experience.

RISK LEADERSHIP

It's clear that recovering from a Risk Hurricane will pose major challenges for any organization. It can be daunting enough simply to "bounce back" to a position where you can restore the previous level of operations, and if you also wish to take the opportunity to conduct a strategic review that might enable you to "bounce forward," then the challenge is magnified even further. Leading your organization through this period will require commitment, patience, persistence, and hard work.

Much has been written about the difference between leadership and management, not all of which is helpful. Table 7.1 provides a summary of the key differences. But the post-Risk Hurricane situation demands a special kind of leadership due to the high levels of uncertainty associated with a Risk Hurricane. This is where we need to demonstrate *risk leadership*, as distinct from risk management.

When the principles of Table 7.1 are applied in situations of extreme risk exposure that might lead to major business disruption, we discover that risk leadership has the following characteristics:

- Risk leaders understand and welcome the uncertain nature of the future, with multiple possible outcomes.

Table 7.1: Leadership and management

Leadership	Management
Leaders have followers.	Managers have subordinates.
Leaders exert influence.	Managers issue instructions.
Leaders demonstrate referent power.	Managers use hierarchical, reward, and sanction power.
Leaders use motivational styles.	Managers use authority-based styles.
Leaders define vision, strategy, and desired outcomes.	Managers execute strategy through tactical action.
Leaders set boundaries.	Managers act within constraints.
Leaders define need for change.	Managers plan and implement change.

- Risk leaders recognize both downside risks (threats) and upside risks (opportunities), and they are determined to take proactive action to minimize threats and maximize opportunities, balancing value protection with value creation.
- Risk leaders are prepared to invest resources in risk management in order to maximize the chances of positive outcomes, even when results are not immediately evident.
- Risk leaders can articulate "How much risk is too much risk" for the business and define the limits of acceptable risk exposure as measurable risk thresholds that express risk appetite.
- Risk leaders encourage appropriate risk-taking within agreed limits.
- Risk leaders demonstrate personal commitment as risk owners by identifying and managing threats and opportunities in their area of responsibility, leading by example, and empowering others to take responsibility for managing risk in their own areas of responsibility.
- Risk leaders understand the strengths and weaknesses of the prevailing risk culture and influence culture change toward a more mature set of beliefs and behaviors.
- Risk leaders recognize that outcomes will not always match plans; some risks will materialize despite people's best efforts, and blame is usually not appropriate.

- Risk leaders welcome those who make them aware of previously unseen risks (including whistle-blowers).
- Risk leaders learn from experience and take action to avoid repeating past mistakes.

If you're a senior risk specialist within your organization, you might already be demonstrating some or all of these risk leadership behaviors and aspiring to others. Your role will include advising your business leadership colleagues on how to act in the unique circumstances that accompany a Risk Hurricane. You might be directly involved in defining potency levels for the types of Risk Hurricane that might affect your organization, monitoring the preconditions to spot the development of possible Risk Hurricanes, building advanced risk models that predict their future track, or advising on appropriate preparedness measures. All of these elements of your risk role are undertaken before the event, and each has a vital part to play in making sure that your leadership colleagues are properly equipped to face an oncoming Risk Hurricane. But your risk expertise is also vital in the post-Risk Hurricane environment, as your organization seeks to recover and rebuild. Your perspective on the key threats and opportunities that lie ahead will provide essential insights to inform strategic decisions on the future direction of the business, influencing the chances of surviving and thriving after a Risk Hurricane.

If you're a senior leader in the business, you may have acquired some practical risk expertise during your journey to the top. It may be the case that your current style includes some risk leadership behaviors, which will help you to lead appropriately in the aftermath of a Risk Hurricane. But your role as business leader is much broader than risk, and it's important that you have expert risk colleagues who can provide the necessary support and input in the risk space at this time of heightened uncertainty.

Both business leaders and risk practitioners should review the characteristics of risk leadership and work together to ensure that all the elements are covered between them. Effective risk leadership will be crucial as you walk through the post-Risk Hurricane landscape, building back and bouncing forward into a changed world.

CASE STUDY: SURVIVING 9/11

On February 26, 1993, terrorists exploded a bomb in the basement of the South Tower of the World Trade Center (WTC) in New York, killing 6 people and injuring over 1,000 others. Financial services firm Dean Witter Morgan Stanley had offices on the upper floors, and staff took four hours to evacuate the building. British-born Rick Rescorla was a corporate security officer for the firm, and in 1997 he recommended that the firm move offices out of the WTC, concerned that another terrorist attack was possible. When that proved impossible, Rescorla and his colleagues developed a detailed disaster recovery and evacuation plan, and he insisted that staff rehearse evacuations every three months.

At 8:46 a.m. on September 11, 2001 (9/11), American Airlines Flight 11 was flown by terrorists into the WTC North Tower. Rescorla was now director of corporate security, and he reacted immediately, implementing a full evacuation of all 2,700 Morgan Stanley staff, who were located across 22 floors high in the WTC South Tower. A second plane struck the South Tower at 9:03 a.m., but most Morgan Stanley staff had already left their offices on higher floors, with all staff evacuated in just 45 minutes. A further 1,000 staff in another WTC building also evacuated successfully. Just 13 Morgan Stanley employees died that morning, sadly including Rick Rescorla, who had reentered the WTC South Tower to check for remaining colleagues just before the building collapsed at 9:59 a.m.

Other elements of the disaster recovery plan were also implemented immediately. By 9:20 a.m., operations staff had activated the IT backup site and had started ordering additional replacement equipment, and senior management established an offsite command center by 9:30 a.m. A call center was transformed into a toll-free emergency hotline by 11 a.m., which started trying to contact all Morgan Stanley employees located in WTC offices. Redundancy in the telecoms infrastructure allowed the company to continue operating, including use of four internet service providers and dedicated emergency telephone lines. Ongoing activities defined in the disaster recovery plan continued until

Morgan Stanley was able to fully resume trading on the New York Stock Exchange on September 17.

Within a few months after 9/11, the company was identifying and documenting lessons to be learned, including the importance of prior contingency planning, regular rehearsal of plans, clear leadership, empowered teams, offsite backups, regular communication, post-event victim support with professional grief/trauma counseling, and proactive rebuilding of corporate identity and community. The disaster recovery plan was reviewed and updated to reflect these learnings.

This brief outline of the Morgan Stanley story clearly indicates several aspects of how to prepare for a Risk Hurricane and what to do in its immediate aftermath. A specific vulnerability assessment had been undertaken between 1990 and 1997, which led to development of detailed short-term proactive preparatory actions and reactive recovery actions that were documented in the disaster recovery plan. In the moment of crisis on 9/11, planned reactive responses were implemented immediately. Empowered staff also took additional action to address issues as they arose. The role played by Rick Rescorla in both planning and execution of the response was the epitome of risk leadership in action.

Longer-term work was undertaken to rebuild the business, with a focus on learning lessons to improve resilience to potential future shocks. But the learning extended well beyond Morgan Stanley. In November 2002 the US National Institute of Standards and Technology (NIST) launched a 3-year, $16 million investigation into the structural failure and progressive collapse of buildings at the WTC. The remit of this investigation was much broader than structural engineering, however, with a dedicated subteam addressing evacuation and emergency communications. Recommendations included changes to building codes, standards, and practices to make buildings safer but also considered elements of human behavior and leadership.

As a result of the 9/11 tragedy, Morgan Stanley emerged as a stronger and more resilient organization (Morgan Stanley, 2021), and their experience informed future good practice in ensuring that other businesses arc better prepared to survive future Risk Hurricanes.

CLOSING CONSIDERATIONS

If your business has experienced the major disruption that comes with a Risk Hurricane, what you do next as a leader in the aftermath will determine the future of your organization. Surviving the immediate chaos of the Risk Hurricane itself is not enough; you need to take action to recover. As you guide your business forward, focus on these three important things:

1. Perform a structured damage assessment, comparing actual outcomes with pre-identified vulnerabilities to find those areas that must be addressed as a priority. Pay particular attention to impacts on people, including your colleagues, other stakeholders, and yourself.
2. Undertake immediate repairs to restore essential functions, including both preplanned reactive responses as well as additional actions to address impacted areas.
3. Map out a path for longer-term rebuilding, considering both the need to bounce back from the impact of major disruption as well as the possibilities to bounce forward to a different and better way of working.

This will require strong, clear, and decisive direction that takes full account of the effects of the uncertainty that you've experienced. Your colleagues will look to you for risk leadership to guide them, learning lessons from your past experience, and positioning the organization to make the most of future challenges and opportunities.

EIGHT

Practicalities

We've come a long way through the preceding chapters, drawing on our rich extended metaphor of the natural hurricane. Along the way, we have:

1. **Presented** the concept of a Risk Hurricane, defining it as "circumstances of extreme risk exposure in business that lead to major disruption"
2. Understood the **preconditions** that allow a Risk Hurricane to form, including a highly uncertain external environment and a weak organizational risk culture, combined with high rates of change
3. Considered how to define a range of **potency** levels for Risk Hurricanes, creating categories that are based on intensity of risk exposure and severity of potential disruption
4. Examined the range of effects a Risk Hurricane can have on **people** in your organization and the wider stakeholder network, both directly and indirectly, as well as outlining the role of professionals
5. Described how to **predict** when a Risk Hurricane is heading your way, the path it might take, and the degree of possible impact it might have, using sophisticated models that provide relevant and accurate information to support effective decision-making

6. Explored how to be as well **prepared** as possible for a Risk Hurricane, including identifying key vulnerabilities then designing both preemptive and reactive measures to protect and recover, as well as longer-term structural changes aimed at improving resilience and developing antifragility within your organization

7. Explained how to design and implement **post-event responses** after a Risk Hurricane has passed, going beyond recovery and rebuilding of preexisting capacity and competence, and actively seeking opportunities to "bounce forward" through disruptive innovation

At every stage, we've aimed to be as practical as possible, and the Closing Considerations section of each chapter has summarized the advice and recommended action points. But as we reach our final chapter, it's time to reemphasize the need to do something different.

CALL TO ACTION

Albert Einstein probably never said, "Insanity is doing the same thing over and over again and expecting different results," but the sentiment is nevertheless true! Another more informal saying that captures the same idea explains that "If we always do what we've always done, we'll always get what we've always got." Having read this far, it's time to put your investment of time and energy to work. If you don't change your thinking or behavior as a result of what you've read, then it's all been for nothing. So here are some final practical suggestions for actions that you might consider:

- *Look out for signs that a Risk Hurricane might arise in or around your business.*
  - ○ Regularly scan the external environment for sources of increasing uncertainty, and closely monitor any developing areas of potential concern.
  - ○ Undertake regular audits of your organizational risk culture and take steps to address any weak or immature areas.
  - ○ Stay aware of changes that might affect your business, noting indications that the rate of change might be rising.

- If/when you spot Risk Hurricane preconditions developing, review your preparedness measures, update and implement preemptive responses, and make sure key colleagues are aware and ready for what might come.
- *Understand what would make a Risk Hurricane more or less severe for your business.*
  - As part of your regular strategic review process, ensure that you understand the organizational risk appetite for each strategic objective, then express this in measurable risk thresholds.
  - Use these risk thresholds to define severity categories for possible degrees of Risk Hurricane impact.
  - Communicate risk thresholds and Risk Hurricane severity categories with key colleagues, encouraging them to develop related lower-level impact definitions across the business.
- *Pay attention to the possible impact of a Risk Hurricane on your stakeholder network*, including business leaders and management, staff at all levels, customers, contractors, suppliers, and other stakeholders.
  - Recognize your particular role in preparing for and tackling a Risk Hurricane. Senior leaders need to be comfortable making risk-intelligent decisions in turbulent times in order to remain within organizational risk capacity. Risk specialists must provide early warning that a Risk Hurricane may be emerging and provide timely and accurate risk information to support decision-makers.
  - Check that you have access to information sources that support effective execution of your role.
  - Provide the necessary support to staff and other stakeholders to enable them to perform their role during a Risk Hurricane.
- *Invest in skills and resources to predict the size and trajectory of a developing Risk Hurricane.*
  - Review the capability and capacity of in-house risk resources to undertake sophisticated and advanced risk analysis, including skills, tools, techniques, and infrastructure. Either take steps to reinforce in-house resources before they're needed or

clarify where the necessary support will be obtained when it is required.

   ○ Consider improving the ability of senior decision-makers to understand how to use risk analysis outputs to support strategic decision-making.

• ***Start now on implementing Risk Hurricane preparedness measures.***

   ○ Review broader organizational culture (not just risk culture) to identify areas that might not be resilient in the event of a Risk Hurricane. Launch a culture change program designed to build resilience, recognizing that this may take several years to reach fruition. Consider opportunities to develop aspects of antifragility into the business.

   ○ Stress-test your strategic objectives to identify areas that would be vulnerable to the extreme risk exposure that comes with a Risk Hurricane.

   ○ Develop and implement proactive preemptive measures to protect vulnerable areas. Design reactive responses to be implemented if/when a Risk Hurricane occurs and ensure prepositioning of required resources. Build both preemptive and reactive actions into your Business Continuity Plan.

• ***Understand what needs to be done after a Risk Hurricane has passed.***

   ○ Design procedures for structured damage assessment, including areas previously identified as vulnerable as well as other affected parts of the business.

   ○ Define responsibilities for immediate post-Risk Hurricane repairs, as well as longer-term rebuilding.

   ○ Consider running simulated exercises to check how well your planned repair and rebuild actions might work.

Our goal has been to provide practical guidance for business leaders and their risk specialist colleagues, giving you the insights, frameworks, and tools that you need to face extreme risk exposure with confidence. The structured list of actions above represents a comprehensive approach to tackling Risk Hurricanes, but the challenge is not trivial. Each bulleted point requires careful thought and consideration, possibly requiring external input, with significant investment of time, effort, and expertise. It's likely that you may not get things right the first time, and an incremental approach may be wise, coming back to check work completed earlier, determining the effectiveness of the approach so far, and making necessary adjustments.

In whatever way you decide to tackle the challenge of taming the Risk Hurricane, it's important to make a start now. Taken together, the actions recommended here provide a robust response to the challenge of extreme risk exposure, giving you and your business the best chance of surviving and thriving the inevitable business disruption that a Risk Hurricane brings.

There's a lot of current discussion at the time of writing about the prospect of significant climate change, one of the likely outcomes of which is predicted to be an increased frequency and severity of natural hurricanes (Studholme et al., 2021).

Perhaps the same might be true of the business environment; maybe the chance of extreme risk exposure that leads to major business disruption is becoming higher? If this turns out to be the case, and Risk Hurricanes are becoming more frequent and more severe, and threatening more areas of business than before, then it is incumbent on all business and risk professionals to be as well prepared as possible. We hope this book will help!

References and Further Reading

ASIS International. (2009). *ASIS SPC.1-2009. Organizational resilience: Security, preparedness and continuity management systems—Requirements with guidance for use.* Alexandria, VA: ASIS International.

Box, G. E. P., & Draper, N. R. (1987). *Empirical model-building and response surfaces.* New York: John Wiley.

British Standards Institute. (2014). *BS 65000:2014. Guidance on organizational resilience.* London: British Standards Institute.

Business Continuity Institute. (2013). *Good practice guidelines.* London: The Business Continuity Institute.

Chapman, R. J. (2011). *Simple tools and techniques for enterprise risk management* (second edition). Chichester, UK: John Wiley.

Churchill, W. S. (1948). *The Second World War, Volume 1: The Gathering Storm.* London: Cassell.

Clark, I. (2016). Business Continuity Management. In D. A. Hillson (Ed.), *The Risk Management Handbook: A practical guide to managing the multiple dimensions of risk.* London: Kogan Page.

Committee of Sponsoring Organizations of the Treadway Commission (COSO). (2017). *Enterprise risk management: Integrating with strategy and performance.* New York: Committee of Sponsoring Organizations of the Treadway Commission.

Deloitte LLP. (2021). *Resilience reimagined: A practical guide for organisations.* London: Deloitte LLP.

Forum for the Future. (n.d.). The Five Capitals. Retrieved December 30, 2021, from https://www.forumforthefuture.org/the-five-capitals.

France24. (n.d.). Bolsonaro's most controversial coronavirus quotes. Retrieved February 28, 2022, from https://www.france24.com/en/live-news/20210619-bolsonaro-s-most-controversial-coronavirus-quotes

Graham, J., & Kaye, D. (2006). *A risk management approach to business continuity: Aligning business continuity with corporate governance.* Brookfield, CT: Rothstein Publishing.

Hillson, D. A. (2002). *Defining professionalism: Introducing the risk management professionalism manifesto.* High Wycombe, UK: Project Management Professional Solutions.

Hillson, D. A. (2003, May). *Defining professionalism in risk management.* Proceedings of PMI Global Congress Europe 2003, The Hague, Netherlands.

Hillson, D. A. (2011a). Enterprise risk management: Managing uncertainty and minimising surprise. In L. Bourne (Ed.), *Advising upwards.* Farnham, UK: Routledge/Gower.

Hillson, D. A. (Ed.). (2011b). *The failure files: Perspectives on failure.* Axminster, UK: Triarchy Press.

Hillson, D. A. (2013, October). *The A-B-C of Risk Culture: How to be Risk-Mature.* Proceedings of PMI Global Congress North America 2013, New Orleans, LA.

Hillson, D. A. (Ed.). (2016). *The Risk Management Handbook: A practical guide to managing the multiple dimensions of risk.* London: Kogan Page.

Hillson, D. A. (2019a). *Capturing upside risk: Finding and managing opportunities in projects.* Boca Raton, FL: Taylor & Francis.

Hillson, D. A. (2019b). Understanding the Risk Mindset. Retrieved December 22, 2021, from https://risk-doctor.com/wp-content/uploads/2020/09/137-The-Risk-Mindset-DH.pdf.

Hillson, D. A. (n.d.). Developing a mature risk mindset. Retrieved February 28, 2022, from https://www.youtube.com/watch?v=ey7yEojNFdE

Hillson, D. A., & Murray-Webster, R. (2007). *Understanding and managing risk attitude* (2nd ed.). Aldershot, UK: Routledge/Gower.

Hillson, D. A., & Murray-Webster, R. (2012). *A short guide to risk appetite.* Aldershot, UK: Routledge/Gower.

House of Lords. (2021). *Preparing for extreme risks: Building a resilient society.* Select Committee on Risk Assessment and Risk Planning. HL Paper 110, Report of Session 2021-22. Retrieved December 24, 2021, from https://publications.parliament.uk/pa/ld5802/ldselect/ldrisk/110/110.pdf

Hulett, D. T. (2011). *Integrated cost-schedule risk analysis.* Farnham, UK: Routledge/Gower.

Institute of Risk Management. (2012). *Risk culture: Resources for practitioners.* London: Institute of Risk Management.

Institute of Risk Management. (2018). *Horizon scanning: A practitioner's guide.* London: Institute of Risk Management.

Institute of Risk Management. (2021). *Organisational resilience: A risk manager's guide.* London: Institute of Risk Management.

Intergovernmental Panel on Climate Change (IPCC). (2005). *Guidance notes for lead authors of the IPCC Fourth Assessment Report on Addressing Uncertainties.* Retrieved December 30, 2021, from https://www.ipcc.ch/site/assets/uploads/2018/02/ar4-uncertaintyguidancenote-1.pdf

Intergovernmental Panel on *Climate Change (IPCC). (2021). Climate Change 2021: The Physical Science Basis. Contribution of Working Group I to the Sixth Assessment Report of the Intergovernmental Panel on Climate Change.* Masson-Delmotte, V., P. Zhai, A. Pirani, S. L. Connors, C. Péan, S. Berger, N. Caud, Y. Chen, L. Goldfarb, M. I. Gomis, M. Huang, K. Leitzell, E. Lonnoy, J.B.R. Matthews, T. K. Maycock, T. Waterfield, O. Yelekçi, R. Yu and B. Zhou (Eds.). Cambridge, UK: Cambridge University Press.

International Organization for Standardization. (2017). *ISO 22316:2017. Security and resilience—Organizational resilience—Principles and attributes.* Geneva, Switzerland: International Organization for Standardization.

International Organization for Standardization. (2018). *ISO 31000:2018. Risk management—Guidelines.* Geneva, Switzerland: International Organization for Standardization.

International Risk Governance Council (IRGC). (2010). *The emergence of risks: Contributing factors.* Geneva, Switzerland: International Risk Governance Council.

International Risk Governance Council (IRGC). (n.d.). Retrieved December 20, 2021, from https://irgc.org/about/

Kipling, R. (1902). *The elephant's child.* In *Just So Stories.* London: Macmillan Publishers Limited.

Mather, J. R. (2005). *Beaufort Wind Scale.* In Oliver J. E. (Ed.), *Encyclopedia of world climatology.* Dordrecht, Netherlands: Springer.

Mayo, J. W. (2017). *Cultural calamity: Culture-driven risk management disasters and how to avoid them.* Arlington, VA: Milton Chadwick & Waters Publishing.

Mayo, J. W. (n.d.). Retrieved February 28, 2022, from http://riskhurricane.com/

Morgan Stanley. (2021). *Reflections on 9/11* (video). Retrieved December 20, 2021, from https://www.morganstanley.com/about-us/history/reflections-on-9-11.

Murray-Webster, R., & Hillson, D. A. (2008). *Managing group risk attitude.* Aldershot, UK: Routledge/Gower.

Murray-Webster, R., & Hillson, D. A. (2021). *Making risky and important decisions: A leader's guide.* Boca Raton, FL: Taylor & Francis.

National Hurricane Center (n.d.a). About the National Hurricane Center. Retrieved December 30, 2021, from https://www.nhc.noaa.gov/aboutintro.shtml.

National Hurricane Center (n.d.b). Saffir-Simpson Hurricane Wind Scale. Retrieved December 30, 2021, from https://www.nhc.noaa.gov/aboutsshws.php.

National Oceanic and Atmospheric Administration (NOAA, n.d.). What is the difference between a hurricane watch and a warning? Retrieved December 30, 2021, from https://oceanservice.noaa.gov/facts/watch-warning.html.

Seville, E. (2016). *Resilient organizations: How to survive, thrive and create opportunities through crisis and change.* London: Kogan Page.

Studholme, J., Fedorov, A. V., Gulev, S. K., Emanuel, K., & Hodges, K. (2021). Poleward expansion of tropical cyclone latitudes in warming climates. *Nature Geoscience*. Retrieved December 29, 2021, from https://doi.org/10.1038/s41561-021-00859-1.

Taleb, N. N. (2007). *The Black Swan: The impact of the highly improbable*. London: Allen Lane/Penguin.

Taleb, N. N. (2012). *Antifragile: Things that gain from disorder*. London: Allen Lane/Penguin.

Taylor, L. (2014). *Practical enterprise risk management: How to optimize business strategies through managed risk-taking*. London: Kogan Page.

United Nations Disaster Risk Reduction (UNDRR). (n.d.). Resilience. Retrieved December 29, 2021, from https://www.undrr.org/terminology/resilience.

Vose, D. (2008). *Risk analysis—A quantitative guide* (3rd ed.). Chichester, UK: John Wiley.

Williams, T. (2002). *Modelling complex projects*. Chichester, UK: John Wiley.

Williams, T. (2007). *Post-project reviews to gain effective lessons learned*. Newtown Square, PA: Project Management Institute.

World Economic Forum (WEF). (2022). *The Global Risks Report 2022* (17th ed.). Geneva, Switzerland: World Economic Forum.

World Economic Forum (WEF). (n.d.). Global risks. Retrieved December 30, 2021, from https://www.weforum.org/global-risks.

World Health Organization (WHO). (n.d.). WHO Coronavirus (COVID-19) Dashboard. Retrieved December 30, 2021, from https://covid19.who.int/.

World Meteorological Organization (WMO). (2012). *Manual on Marine Meteorological Services: Volume I–Global Aspects (WMO-No. 558)*. Geneva, Switzerland: World Meteorological Organization.

World Meteorological Organization (WMO). (n.d.). World weather watch. Retrieved December 30, 2021, from https://public.wmo.int/en/programmes/world-weather-watch.

Index

Page references with an f refer to figures, those with a t refer to tables.

About the Author

Known globally as The Risk Doctor, Dr David Hillson is a leading thinker and expert practitioner with a well-deserved reputation as an excellent speaker and presenter on risk. His talks blend thought-leadership with practical application, presented in an accessible style that combines clarity with humor, guided by the Risk Doctor motto: "Understand profoundly so you can explain simply."

During his 35-year international consulting career leading The Risk Doctor Partnership, David has advised major organizations, governments, and charities in nearly 60 countries on how to create value from risk using applied risk-based thinking, and his wisdom and insights are in high demand. He is currently making his legacy available through speaking and writing so that others can build on the foundation he leaves behind.

David has developed a range of significant innovations in the way risk is understood and managed, many of which are now accepted as best practice. As well as publishing major books on risk (13 so far), David regularly shares his work through the RiskDoctorVideo YouTube channel, with over 200 videos and more than 1.5 million views.

David has received many awards for his groundbreaking work in risk management. He is a Fellow of the Institute of Risk Management (IRM), a Fellow of the Project Management Institute (PMI), and an Honorary Fellow of the UK Association for Project Management (APM). He can be contacted at david@risk-doctor.com.

Berrett–Koehler
Publishers

Berrett-Koehler is an independent publisher dedicated to an ambitious mission: *Connecting people and ideas to create a world that works for all.*

Our publications span many formats, including print, digital, audio, and video. We also offer online resources, training, and gatherings. And we will continue expanding our products and services to advance our mission.

We believe that the solutions to the world's problems will come from all of us, working at all levels: in our society, in our organizations, and in our own lives. Our publications and resources offer pathways to creating a more just, equitable, and sustainable society. They help people make their organizations more humane, democratic, diverse, and effective (and we don't think there's any contradiction there). And they guide people in creating positive change in their own lives and aligning their personal practices with their aspirations for a better world.

And we strive to practice what we preach through what we call "The BK Way." At the core of this approach is *stewardship,* a deep sense of responsibility to administer the company for the benefit of all of our stakeholder groups, including authors, customers, employees, investors, service providers, sales partners, and the communities and environment around us. Everything we do is built around stewardship and our other core values of *quality, partnership, inclusion,* and *sustainability.*

This is why Berrett-Koehler is the first book publishing company to be both a B Corporation (a rigorous certification) and a benefit corporation (a for-profit legal status), which together require us to adhere to the highest standards for corporate, social, and environmental performance. And it is why we have instituted many pioneering practices (which you can learn about at www.bkconnection.com), including the Berrett-Koehler Constitution, the Bill of Rights and Responsibilities for BK Authors, and our unique Author Days.

We are grateful to our readers, authors, and other friends who are supporting our mission. We ask you to share with us examples of how BK publications and resources are making a difference in your lives, organizations, and communities at www.bkconnection.com/impact.

Dear reader,

Thank you for picking up this book and welcome to the worldwide BK community! You're joining a special group of people who have come together to create positive change in their lives, organizations, and communities.

What's BK all about?

Our mission is to connect people and ideas to create a world that works for all.

Why? Our communities, organizations, and lives get bogged down by old paradigms of self-interest, exclusion, hierarchy, and privilege. But we believe that can change. That's why we seek the leading experts on these challenges—and share their actionable ideas with you.

A welcome gift

To help you get started, we'd like to offer you a **free copy** of one of our bestselling ebooks:

www.bkconnection.com/welcome

When you claim your **free ebook**, you'll also be subscribed to our blog.

Our freshest insights

Access the best new tools and ideas for leaders at all levels on our blog at ideas.bkconnection.com.

Sincerely,

Your friends at Berrett-Koehler